Bertha Beachy

Desiring

Desiring Life

BENEDICT ON WISDOM AND THE GOOD LIFE

Norvene Vest

COWLEY PUBLICATIONS
Cambridge · Boston
Massachusetts

Published in the United States of America by Cowley Publications, a division of the Society of St. John the Evangelist. No portion of this book may be reproduced, stored in or introduced into a retrieval system, or transmitted, in any form or by any means—including photocopying—without the prior written permission of Cowley Publications, except in the case of brief quotations embedded in critical articles and reviews.

Library of Congress Cataloging-in-Publication Data:
Vest, Norvene.
    Desiring Life: Benedict on wisdom and the good life / by Norvene Vest.
    p. cm.
    Includes bibliographical references.
    ISBN: 1-56101-182-7
    1. Benedictines—Spiritual life. 2. Monastic and religious life.
    I. Title.
BX3003 .V47 2000
248.4'82—dc21   00-43192

Scripture quotations are from the *New Revised Standard Version of the Bible,* © 1989 by the Division of Christian Education of the National Council of the Churches of Christ in the USA. Used by permission. All rights reserved.

Editor: Cynthia Shattuck; Copyeditor and Designer: Vicki Black
Cover art: detail of Kerman Ravar carpet, late 19th century

This book was printed in Canada by Transcontinental Printing on recycled, acid-free paper.

Cowley Publications
28 Temple Place • Boston, Massachusetts 02111
800-225-1534 • www.cowley.org

I wish to thank the growing number of
Benedictines, especially women, who grace my
life with wisdom and love.
And to the ongoing inner struggle,
the disequilibrium and confusion out of which
new life emerges for me and for many of us,
thanks be to god.

Table of Contents

Acknowledgments

S pecial thanks to Fr. Luke Dysinger, OSB and to Source Books for allowing me to use Fr. Luke's new translation of the Rule of St. Benedict, which closely follows the original Latin and produces a text that readily demonstrates Benedict's changes from his older source, the *Rule of the Master.*

Desire as Problem
or Promise

*Is there anyone who yearns for life and desires to
see good days?*

This verse fragment paraphrased from the opening
paragraphs of the Rule of St. Benedict is God's call to
each one of us every day of our lives: "Do you yearn for
life?" If our answer is "Yes, I do!" then God will show us
the way of life.

Sometime after the beginning of the sixth century C.E.,
the abbot of a mountaintop monastery in Italy wrote
down his practical wisdom about the living of a full
human life, assuring his readers that God's desire was that
we find the way to fullness of life. The abbot was Benedict
of Nursia; the writings are called his "Rule." The next
thousand years are sometimes called the "Benedictine centuries" because of the widespread and civilizing impact of
the Rule of Benedict. Even today, monastics live and work
under the humane standards of that same Rule.

Benedictines are sometimes thought of as those who leave the world behind, taking stringent vows and living behind high walls. However, in the last decade we have seen a remarkable growth of interest in Benedictine wisdom by people who do not aspire to cloister life. Many ordinary folks living in this new century sense that the Rule may be a helpful guide as we endeavor to live a full human life. Living a full human life: this sounds like a dream to many of us, seen more clearly in automobile advertisements than in the actual experience of anyone we know. What do we imagine it might mean to live a full life? Is that a promise in which we dare to believe?

Occasionally in our quiet moments, many of us wonder, What is the purpose of human life anyway? What are the possibilities? We see people making fabulous incomes as professional athletes or stock market wizards, yet money does not seem to buy them happiness. Observing the recent mad scrambles of politicians in Washington, we can conclude that having power may not be satisfying in and of itself. The media reports on the lives of the young and the beautiful seldom offer us compelling role models. Where do we look to find reasons for our existence?

Disappointed in external standards, we may turn inward, asking ourselves what we think will fulfill us. What is it that we really desire? We have many different desires, and because some of them have led us astray from time to time we have learned not to trust our own instincts as reliable guides to fullness of life. And yet at quiet moments we can still hear the faint cry of an inner restlessness that will not let us settle for things as they are. "Surely there is more than this to life!" "It's probably foolish, but I feel I'm made for something great, something special and unique, and I know that as yet I have not found it." "I cannot *name* it, but some inner longing keeps drawing me toward it." Sometimes we find something we think is "the answer"—a relationship, a job, a spiritual

2

practice but eventually we find that it, too, is only part of what we are searching for, and the longing returns.

As a society we may not yet have realized how serious a problem our unrequited desires for fullness of life really are. The utterly personal and deeply interior hunger for purpose is echoed and magnified in the culture at large, as people try to mask their despair of finding life with a purpose given the cynicism and hopelessness of our world. We have the power to destroy our planet and often seem perilously close to exercising that power; we no longer expect our air or water or foods to be free of pollutants. Many young adults today have watched their parents work themselves into early graves and abandon families in the course of midlife crises, and they are reluctant to make any commitments. Through our daily experience of television, we are more aware than ever of the severe poverty and despair of peoples all over the world, yet we are overwhelmed by the scope of the suffering and so do nothing.

The truth is that we live in a transition time, a time we might think of as the crumbling of civilization as we have known it. We do not share the common moral foundations upon which virtue and ethics can be enacted. We lack wisdom about the way to a supremely fulfilling life. We have no common perspective on what it is to be human. At some level we are aware of a pervasive sense of being adrift, having lost our fundamental connections, but we do not know how to begin afresh, even if we recognize the current transitional time as bearing the potential for transformation.

My thesis in this book is that the desire for fullness of life is primarily a longing for a meaningful relationship with God. If humans beings are created for intimate union with something quite beyond and other than themselves, then our restlessness cannot be eased until we feel the nearness of God. However, our images of God often prevent us from experiencing the presence we long for. We

3

have come to see that God is not an old man on a white throne who is untouched by human suffering; nor is God the stern and judgmental controller of all human actions. Yet the collapse of such images has left a void in our ways of thinking about God, for a sense of intimate union with the Divine is impossible without a personal connectedness and a vital interchange with Mystery itself. Christian scriptures confirm the reality of an ongoing and personal relationship between the Divine and human beings, but the language used to describe that relationship often seems irrelevant to modern experience. We need the means to translate traditional faith into contemporary language, contemporary lives.

The task of translation in our time is compounded by the presence of three powerful and interrelated biases now deeply rooted in our culture, all of which are strongly identified with self-reliance. We could call those biases "cultural blinkers"—outdated paradigms so widespread as to be effectively invisible. They are:

1. The lack of a coherent language for dialogue about the meaning of life;

2. An exaggerated reliance on "results"; and

3. A delight in mocking the tender and the cherished.

Each of these three pervasive modes of thinking will be described and examined in the following chapters, as we endeavor to contrast each with a perspective from the Christian monastic tradition that challenges it. The Rule of Benedict and the traditions that shaped Benedict's thinking will be our sources for discovering and recovering new images of fullness of life and relationship with God.

First we will examine the wisdom tradition of scripture, which Benedict clearly adopted as his own, offering wisdom as a way to recover a coherent language of meaning. Our hunger for life is foundational. We desire to live fully and well, honoring all the dimensions of our being, while respecting other beings with whom we share this planet, and serving God with gladness. As the wisdom traditions and Benedict ponder how to be faithful to this basic human desire, they inevitably engage two other central human concerns.

What sort of persons should we try to become?—this is the question of virtue. In part two we will look at the tradition of virtue, especially in the early monastic desert experience, emphasizing the development of personal integrity or character rather than reliance upon "utility" or results as a primary measure of human value.

What action do we take as wise persons? What are our practical relationships with the rest of the created order with other humans, creatures, and the earth? This is the question of ethics, which we will explore in part three. We will look particularly at Benedict's list of Instruments of Good Works as a skillful and relevant description of ethics that sees our actions as the fruit of the divine-human union and offers us a foundation for daily decisions directed toward ultimate values.

In each part of this book we take one chapter of the Rule that seems most directly to address the issue at hand. Chapter two on wisdom reviews Benedict's Prologue verse by verse, in which Benedict articulates his perspective on what human life is all about, what we are here for, what we are meant to do. The chapters on virtue review Benedict's chapter seven on humility, which is a compact summary of his spiritual theology, elaborated in his first six chapters. Our chapter six on ethics reviews Benedict's chapter four on the instruments of good works, which is a succinct expression of the spiritual tradition Benedict inherits from scripture and the early fathers and mothers of the church. These are possibly the three pivotal chapters in the Rule, but because they are highly condensed and deal with unfamiliar concepts, they are not easy for us to understand. So we will take some time with them,

5

imagining and exploring and endeavoring to "translate" how their principles speak to us in our current need.

All six chapters of this book contrast our modern outlook with the Christian tradition as practiced by the Benedictines. Wisdom reveals itself in our virtue and our ethics, or not at all. In order to appreciate the ancient tradition anew, we must notice how the limiting biases of recent centuries prevent us from genuine receptivity to the past. Having seen the present clearly, we are free to create a more adequate synthesis of the best of the old with the best of the new. But seeing the present clearly may at first only deepen our discouragement. Like that crucial moment in a board game, many people today have a strong sense that all the signs point toward disaster. Do we give up then and there? Do we play it out to the bitter end? Or is there any chance to shift strategies mid-game to retrieve what looks like sure loss?

What it means to be human in God's world is that we *can* shift strategies—not just in a board game, but in life itself. Knowledge and courage are required, as are a sense of urgency and a commitment to the work. The crucial addition to these qualities is a shift in perspective. We can suddenly "wake up" to a new perspective on what is happening. Whereas only a moment before everything looked grim for us, a sudden insight can reveal an obvious play that will suddenly turn the tables. When we feel stuck, the problem is often that we are looking at things too narrowly. Another way of seeing, even from long ago, can often bring new promise.

The power of internal perspective is conveyed in one of my favorite stories about a young girl called Suzie who spent a few hours each week delivering doughnuts for her uncle, the baker. Unfortunately, the child had a bad habit of eating the goods before making her deliveries. Trying to outwit the girl, one day the uncle sent her out to deliver a box of nine doughnuts, on the top of which he had clearly marked a large Roman numeral IX. Yet as soon as Suzie was out of sight of the bakery, she gobbled down three of the doughnuts before she knew it! She discovered a pencil in her pocket, but no eraser. Thinking quickly, she added a single mark to the box top and completed her assignment with the same number inside and out. What did Suzie do?

7

Think about it a moment. Note that this is not a problem in moral theology, but only one of perception, or vision. The story itself establishes the perspective, or mind-set, of numbers. If you try to solve the problem with Roman numerals or even Arabic numbers, the problem is insoluble. However, if you are able to challenge the internal perspective or the given "set" as Suzie did when she thought of *letters*, the immediately obvious answer is to add an "s" in front of the "IX", making SIX.

I love this story because it shows so clearly what it is like to be stuck in a problem until a simple shift of focus reveals an obvious solution. The point is that we always bring to our experience a certain framework or way of looking at things, and that framework both *helps* us see and *limits* what we are able to see. So often the truth, or the way through to creative new possibilities, can be found only when we abandon our existing perceptual framework, allowing a new and more adequate one to form in our minds and hearts.

In the doughnut story the set perspective is short-term and individual, but in the overall issues of concern to us the set perspective is more serious, because it is long-term and deeply woven into the web of our common expectations as a society. Each of us is shaped by our culture's views of what is possible and what is not, what is important and what is not. We all are influenced to some degree by the perspective of the society in which we have been formed. The broad cultural perspective in which we live contributes to our pervasive fear and despair, and tends to prevent our receptivity to experiences that would help us regain faith and hope.

Every person acts from some framework of faith, whether it be that the sun will rise each morning and darkness fall at night or that scientific hypotheses can be tested by experiment and observation. Both are matters of faith. But today our cultural limits frequently encourage us to discount experiences that an older tradition called the presence of God. The three cultural biases we will discuss—no common language of meaning, over-reliance on results, and disdain for altruistic values—tragically collaborate to make any notion of God seem like a private, self-induced fantasy. Hope always moves forward to things unseen, uncertain, and not now present. But our future is cut off when we no longer allow ourselves to hope for intimacy with God.

Recovery of Benedict's vital tradition is a way to recast the problem of our unfulfilled longing for life. When recast, the problem can become a promise of new possibilities. The time now may be exactly ripe for a new vision, just as it was in Benedict's day. After the fall of Rome in 410 C.E., a distressing loss of the old values was also evident. Fear and despair were more frequent companions than faith and hope among the population at large, even as an authentic spiritual hunger gained strength in some people. Likewise, in our own day we see a widespread distress accompanied by a dramatic increase in the demand for "spiritual" books. Growing numbers of people are testing a wide range of methods purporting to offer wisdom and an experience of a transcendent presence radically different from what our senses or rational minds can provide.

The hunger for what might be called "mystical" or direct experience of God is expanding, along with an awareness that it probably requires a mature ascetical discipline to support ongoing communion at that level. The

8

mystical dimension might be called the consciousness of God's active presence in time and space. The ascetical dimension then could be understood as a realistic framework to shape our own human action and presence in time and space. How does God act? How shall we act? These are the two questions at the foundation of the spiritual life indeed, of all human life.

Can we restore these essential elements of human life in ways that are realistic enough to deal with suffering and cynicism while also vital and engaging enough to inspire and sustain? This book argues that we can indeed bring about such a restoration, by creating a synthesis of the strengths of our period with the strengths of an older one. We know that such a restoration will not be simple, for our current condition must be addressed with sufficient power to coax forth a renewal of faith and hope. Yet we can turn to traditional sources with the confidence that early Christians understood both human nature and social constraints far better than we might imagine, and that their wisdom is sturdy enough to create a strong and viable "hybrid" to fortify and renew us. The promise of the past is rich with possibilities for us.

This book is intended as the third in my series on Benedictine spirituality for contemporary life. All three books complement one another and are necessary supplements in understanding the whole Benedictine vision. *No Moment Too Small* focuses on the foundational elements of silence, holy reading *(lectio divina)*, and prayer. *Friend of the Soul* discusses the integration of work and faith. And this book explores the meaning and fullness of human life, as understood in the gospel and lived in ongoing relationship to the God of Christ. All are meant to help with specific choices in daily living. As you read and pray, may you find Benedict's promise fulfilled, and your heart opened wide in the unspeakable sweetness of love (RB Prologue 49).

PART ONE

Wisdom

CHAPTER 1

Desiring Life

Does not wisdom call?...Take my instruction instead of silver, and knowledge rather than choice gold; for wisdom is better than jewels, and all that you may desire cannot compare with her....Happy is the one who listens to me, watching daily at my gates, waiting beside my doors. For whoever finds me finds life. (Proverbs 8:1, 10-11, 34-35)

L ife is more than food and drink. We breathe, eat, sleep, and work, knowing that life is more than these. We seek inner coherence, a narrative thread, something that gives us a sense that our lives matter, that there is meaning to what we do. We know that we will die, and we want to know that there is a purpose to our living. At times we may experience life as squeezed dry or closed in. We may find ourselves asking, "Is this all there is?" On the surface things are fine, but a small voice inside weeps: surely we were not born only for this dogged routine. We may "wake up" suddenly in the midst of rush-hour traffic, wondering how we got to this joyless place. We have a sense that something eludes us, yet we cannot cease to long for it. There is nothing particularly wrong with the way things are, yet all is not quite right. Something essential is still lacking.

14

Sometimes, in contrast, we feel directly connected to a quality of "knowing." In a moment of illumination, we feel ourselves full to overflowing with gladness, centered in a sense of utter *rightness*. Everything seems to be in tune—the time and the place, the people and the activity, the resources and the need—and we are uplifted beyond imagining. The inner voices sing, and we feel we were made for this moment. Possibly we have just fallen in love, and it seems that we are seeing sunsets as they were meant to be for the first time, so arrayed are they with vibrant color. Or perhaps we are closing a fellowship gathering with people we have known for many years, and we are reluctant to leave the evening because the interaction among us has been so honest, so full of compassion and vulnerability, so marked by mutual care.

Most lives contain a mixture of both kinds of moments, but we intuitively associate the latter feeling with life and the former with death. We long to feel more and more in accord with *life*. The wise among us are those who desire life abundant, and have found the way to it. In this chapter we will explore the wisdom tradition, and Benedict's use of it, as a model that reaches both backward and forward to create a cohesive language full of grace and meaning for our times.

Human wisdom is rooted in the deep desire of our hearts to live fully into the promise of our being. Wisdom seeks life that is really life—life that is blessing, life that is abundant. This kind of life may mean something different to each of us. Some might associate it with the great peace when the lion lies down with the lamb. Some might dream of justice and mutual respect freely shared among all people and creatures. For some, fullness of life may suggest freedom to work seriously in life's vocation, or to worship without fear.

This desire for fullness of life is not new. Our scriptures are full of searching for life and the way to it, especially in the wisdom literature—those books concerned with the big questions of life. The Proverbs quotation that begins this chapter expresses a deep yearning for life that also has a practical edge. Proverbs and the other books of the wisdom tradition probe the difference between choices that lead toward life and those that bring spiritual and psychic dying instead. Many passages reveal the contrast between motives and moments that seem to fulfill human capacities and others that narrow them:

15

> And now, my children, listen to me: happy are those who keep my ways. Hear instruction and be wise, and do not neglect it. . . . For whoever finds me finds life and obtains favor from the LORD; but those who miss me injure themselves; all who hate me love death. (Proverbs 8:32-33, 35-36)

> Do you not know this from of old, ever since mortals were placed on earth, that the exulting of the wicked is short, and the joy of the godless is but for a moment? (Job 20:4-5)

Wisdom is always asking what it means to be a human being and to what sort of life we are called. Humans are creatures, earth-bound and constrained by limits of space and time. Yet we also know ourselves to be *more* than mere creatures, urged always somehow to share the divine life, to transcend ourselves in some mysterious way. Wisdom seeks to understand this paradox and to find the way to experiencing life in abundance.

Yet the advice of the sages tends to be pragmatic and reasonable. They are not so much interested in what *should* be as in what *is*, based on their observations of people and their actions in the context of the mysterious Blessing undergirding all things. For the sages life is more than simple material success, yet they do not separate the created world from God's blessing and purpose. Wisdom's sages seek to identify reliable patterns within the daily round, but they are keenly aware of the limitations of human knowledge and of the inevitable mystery of God's activity in creation. We are often frustrated by the sages because they refuse to relinquish either side of an unsettling tension between the tangible and the intangible. They might never fully understand the mechanics of the continuous web of Spirit and world, but they are convinced that human life is fundamentally relational; love of God is intimately linked both with the quality of daily routine and with the desire to become more whole.

The Judeo-Christian tradition of wisdom is not particularly systematic. While wisdom is centered in a search for the hidden order of things, it makes that journey in a mode we would call "subjective"—that is, wisdom is experiential, based on inward rumination, and relational. It is not only a collection of ideas and values, but also a particular way of thinking and knowing. The ancient art of wisdom anticipates the "new physics" in its insight that fullness of life cannot be approached from the "outside," as a disinterested observer. Just to *observe* reality is to change it. Because the created world is God's, and the desire for life is a quality given to humans by God in creation, ultimately there is no "outside." Our deepest longings tell us something true about the nature of reality.

∽ The Lack of a Common Language
A striking characteristic of our time is that we are uncomfortable engaging in serious dialogue about subjective, intangible values. Public and private conversation tends to be confined to "objective" matters: to data, to information, to details. Anything intangible is considered mere

opinion; everyone is entitled to his or her own opinion, but we tend to believe there is no effective way to communicate deeply with another person about matters of spiritual, religious, and moral experience. We are aptly captured in Yeats' well-known line from "The Second Coming": "The best lack all conviction, while the worst are full of passionate intensity." The passionate intensity of superficial personal opinion embarrasses us, but people of deep reflection seldom either make public commitments or speak of them to others.

17

On the whole, our language gives us few ways to express our wonder, beauty, integrity—those things that lack objective, quantifiable verification. Without a more expressive yet relevant language, we are unable to acknowledge meaning and purpose in human life. Scientific and technical language avowedly has no tools to speak of meaning and purpose—such matters are beyond their scope of concern. But when most public discourse takes place within the framework of technical language, our conversation becomes increasingly narrow, and life is diminished. All truly important matters—the beautiful, the tender, the good—transcend the literal, so they are discounted. We have reached the point in this dismaying sequence of thought where many people no longer even dare hope that there is such a thing as meaning or fullness in human life.

This state of affairs is tragic. Without meaning, human beings cut themselves off from an essential connection to life. We are made for meaning, just as we are made with an apparent desire for God—the More Than We Are. When religious and ascetical values are suppressed, the hunger for meaning spurts out in random and unexpected ways, as we see in the avid consumption of almost anything claiming to offer "spiritual" wisdom, or in the increase of physical violence that at least momentarily gives some individuals a sense of being truly alive, powerful and full of adrenaline. We see just how far we are from genuine wisdom both in the effort to "buy" it from the latest fad and in the desperate longing to feel *anything,* even when it harms ourselves and others.

I believe that a major reason for our lack of a rich and vibrant spirit of wisdom today is the loss of a coherent, common language for dialogue about the meaning of life. To be coherent means to be logically or aesthetically ordered or integrated, something that hangs together firmly as parts of the same unit or mass. Today we have pieces of language about meaning, partial and fragmented symbols, that emerge randomly in conversation. The occurrence of these words and symbols, even their frequent occurrence, may encourage us to believe that such a language is available to us. But a close look at *how* such language is used reveals that the words and symbols themselves are used to negate rather than affirm meaning.

In a recent keynote address at a conference on monastic life, church sociologist Scott Appleby recounted his experience of writing a paper in his study at home while his youngest child watched television in an adjacent room. He was researching an ancient Latin phrase expressing the consensus of a major church council, and suddenly he heard the exact phrase spoken on his son's television program. Startled, he realized that the Latin was being used as a magical gibberish phrase in children's entertainment; later he learned the program script writer had majored in classics in college. Appleby pointed out that when once-meaningful symbols are used in a random and fragmented way, they are stripped of the power they carried in context.

Symbol fragments persist in the culture after their embedded meaning is lost. We might think of the cross as the symbol which above all expresses a cohesive statement of Christian meaning, but its trivialization in today's secular culture suggests that even such a once-powerful symbol is no longer coherent. There was a time when crosses were desecrated *because* of their power—that is, lost souls oppressed by the power of Christ's cross for transformation might break or burn a cross in an effort to drive its call from their consciousness. But what we see recently is not that: today the symbol of the cross can be used with indifference or ignorance. The very successful stage play *Phantom of the Opera,* for example, does try to grapple with themes of light and darkness, goodness and evil. But in a pivotal scene showing the Phantom departing from a graveyard hiding place, he emerges from behind a giant gateway cross that was used merely a dramatic stage prop, only barely evoking a once-potent memory of the ultimacy of divine redemption. In another example, the popular performance artist Marilyn Manson (a man) recently entered a tour concert dressed only in a black silken jock strap and black feather boa, his semi-nude body affixed to a huge, rolling, metalworked cross. Manson and his reviewers made no reference to his "conveyance" during or after the performance; it was merely a rather startling way to get on stage.

19

People who have been taught the full richness and coherence of the Christian story may be offended or alarmed by such trivialization of sacred symbols. But there are fewer and fewer such people among us, even in the ranks of regular churchgoers. For as Appleby points out, in the tumultuous 1960s many young people refused systematic religious teaching as irrelevant, and never thought to transmit it to their own (now newly adult) children. People whose understanding of the faith is merely rote or barely comprehensive are not distressed by the deterioration of once-powerful symbols because they did not understand the connections to deep human meaning in the first place.

In *After Virtue* Alasdair MacIntyre offers a parable to help us see our situation.[1] He asks that we imagine a catastrophe overtaking the natural sciences. After a sequence of environmental disasters, which have been blamed on the scientific community, a popular uprising occurs in which most scientific laboratories, books, and instruments are destroyed and some scientists killed. A populist government then successfully abolishes science teaching in the schools and its reporting in the media. When people try to revive science generations later, they have largely forgotten what it was. All they possess are fragments: a few instruments whose use has been forgotten; half-chapters from books torn and charred. Nonetheless, all these fragments are collected and taught under the old and now revived names of physics, chemistry, and biology, though the content of what is being taught bears little resemblance to real science, for the contexts that might make sense of the fragments have been lost, perhaps irretrievably. Yet those trying to revive the ancient wisdom would not realize that they were presenting merely an empty shadow of the real thing.

MacIntyre's point is that just such a situation exists in the present world of morality (and I would add, of religious meaning). We possess only fragments—words and symbols without contexts. We still have expressions, but their significance has been lost. And we do not recognize the enormity of our incapacity, instead blaming the morality itself for being meaningless to us.

We retain words and expressions that should carry meaning, but because they are deprived of their context they actually contribute to our growing suspicion of meaninglessness. Responding to this situation, two rival groups seem to have emerged. Some seek to identify certain truths and eliminate all doubt, clinging to literal religious language. In contrast, others eager for novelty consider traditional religious language—and especially biblical admonitions—to be merely outdated historical baggage. Yet neither approach has addressed the underly-

20

ing issue of the lack of a common, coherent language about the purpose of life. Neither is satisfying and responsive to the spiritual hunger so many of us feel.

Clearly, we lack a robust, powerful, relevant language of public discourse about morality, about wisdom, about the fullness of human life for which we are meant. We have only the default languages of economics and politics, neither of which encompasses genuine community. We can readily speak about "bottom lines" and "voter concerns" and "environmental hazards." But we scarcely know what words to use to talk of experiences of divine presence, of our deep longings of the heart, of our struggles to live with integrity. The more acutely we feel this loss, the more urgently do we seek potential resources. Indigenous cultures attract us by their uncomplicated connection to earth. Feminist circles offer ways to embody Spirit, in shared worship and embrace of the sensual. Eastern religions practice ancient methods of breathing, quieting, and oneness with Being which assuage the heart's hunger. Yet none of these offers the common language we seek.

Meanwhile, a few persistent and flexible explorers have turned back to earlier centuries of Christian experience, seeking to recover the lost connections and contexts. They are uncovering a rich and powerful heritage that is able to serve the needs of varying times and cultures. We can benefit from the explorations of Alasdair MacIntyre and Stanley Hauerwas in moral theology, of Roberta Bondi and Peter Brown as historians of the spirit of the early church, of women like Esther de Waal and Kathleen Norris and a growing numbers of Benedictine authors including Joan Chittister, Columba Stewart, and Katherine Howard—who are contributing to the recovery of that vital and wise heritage. Many of us today are finding in the Rule of Benedict—itself a response to living out the gospel in a time of evolving needs and loss of tradi-

21

tional contexts of meaning—an enormously helpful entry into the wisdom embedded in the Christian tradition.

Wisdom itself depends upon a search both of experience and tradition, blending the best of both, integrating the insights of the past with the possible strengths of the future, or as Benedict says, knowing how to "bring forth new things and old" (RB 64:9, based on Matthew 13:52). Whenever people search for the keys to fullness of life, particular themes seem to emerge over and over, a set of core values so foundational they are sometimes called the "perennial philosophy." The Christian faith tradition has traced out these perennial values no less profoundly than other sources and they are largely embedded in what we call the wisdom tradition. St. Benedict clearly saw himself as a link in this chain of ongoing wisdom flowing from the God of Abraham and Sarah through the God of Jesus Christ and at last, to us. This wisdom offers a cohesive language of grace and meaning to help us live well and fully in our times.

❧ Themes of the Wisdom Tradition

There are three books of wisdom in the Hebrew Bible—Ecclesiastes, Job, and Proverbs—and two from the Apocrypha: The Wisdom of Solomon (Wisdom) and Ecclesiasticus (or the Wisdom of Jesus Son of Sirach). Sections of other Old Testament books are also regarded as part of the wisdom corpus, including the narrative "Joseph story" in Genesis (about a "wise" life) and portions of the Psalms; it has even influenced segments of the Pauline letters.[2] Wisdom writings are recognizable through their theme of the search for, and lessons about, a full human life. Proverbs immediately states its purpose as being "for learning about wisdom and instruction, for understanding words of insight, for gaining instruction in wise dealing, righteousness, justice, and equity" (Proverbs 1:2-3). The underlying concern always seems to be, "How can a person live wisely and well?" For example, Ecclesiastes states clearly, "I searched ... until I might see what was good for mortals to do under heaven" (2:3). In the midst of great suffering Job cries out to God, "Why did you bring me forth from the womb?" (10:18). And the Wisdom of Solomon affirms, "God created us for incorruption, and made us in the image of his own eternity" (2:23).

23

Another key trait of a wisdom text is that it frequently promises an insight into fullness of life, using an introductory formula like the following:

> My child, keep my words and store up my commandments with you: keep my commandments and live, keep my teachings as the apple of your eye; bind them on your fingers, write them on the tablet of your heart." (Proverbs 7:1-3)

For our wise ancestors, the most important aspect of parenting was to teach children to live fully and well. Even more important than physical care, food, and shelter, the work of the parent was to transmit wisdom. Spiritual elders were those entrusted with the forming of character that is attuned to the ways of God and the inner structure of created reality. Benedict himself lets us know that in writing his Rule, he is joining the ranks of wisdom teachers, beginning his prologue with just these words, "Listen O my child to the precepts of an old one, and incline the ear of your heart" (RB Prologue 1, paraphrased).

The oldest of the three primary wisdom books, the book of Proverbs, consists mainly of short sayings in the form of similitudes that reveal practical wisdom in famliar concepts. The goal is to stimulate a delighted recognition of the way things are, so the listener is moved to live according to a discovery about God's purpose implanted in creation itself. We may at first be put off by the fact that the proverbs concern practical knowledge. Wisdom starts in the basic experience of mastering life. "The plans of the diligent lead surely to abundance, but everyone who is hasty comes only to want" (Proverbs 21:5) is a characteristic couplet, urging diligence and condemning haste. Mastery concerns not so much control of events, for the wise know that is beyond human ability, but rather learning to live in harmony with an underlying life embedded within creation. In the context of such apparently minor and practical observations, wisdom builds toward a life of righteousness, of integrity toward the divine Creator. Wisdom is set in contrast to folly, or more aptly, wickedness. But the true opposite to wisdom is actually inattention and indifference, a dullness of spirit that has no vital questions to put to its environment.

24

Nowadays we imagine order to be the antithesis of chaos or surprise. But this is a proposition contrary to the spirit of wisdom. Although they were seeking to discern a hidden order in things and events, the early sages were not distressed or derailed by the discovery of paradox. For example, while we are to seek wisdom with all our strength ("Fools think their own way is right, but the wise listen to advice." Proverbs 12:15), in a certain sense wisdom is always elusive, always hidden in the mind of God, and our search for wisdom cannot make us God's equal: "No wisdom, no understanding, no counsel, can avail against the Lord" (Proverbs 21:30). The point of wisdom is not to demand literal obedience but rather to invite the listener to test it against one's own observations and life experience. It endeavors to throw light upon details as potentially revealing the sacred, and to puzzle a person into deeper reflection on things that might have been too quickly dismissed.

The book of Job directly addresses the question so much on our minds today, of why bad things happen to good people. The unexplained suffering of innocent children or generous and loving adults poses a direct chal-

lenge to our sense of how things should be. We would like
to be certain that living a wholesome life eliminate problems or suffering. But wisdom is more elusive than that.
God's ways are not our ways, and the moment we think
we fully understand God's order, something disruptive
happens and the mystery of apparent chaos confronts us
anew. Job fleshes out the simpler world view of Proverbs,
testing the basic belief in a reliable underlying order of
things.

In general, Proverbs makes the case for what is called
retributive justice: you deserve what you get. It observes
that the foolish and wicked are punished, whereas the
wise and righteous are rewarded. But Job takes the argument one step further, showing that sometimes even the
righteous seem to be punished. Job's "friends" keep trying
to make him admit that he must have sinned against God,
thus causing all the disasters that befell him. But Job will
not bow to conventional wisdom, holding fast instead to
his own inner experience of fidelity. While the prologue
tells us that Job will not curse God (Job 2:3), the story
itself reveals otherwise. Job blames God for treating him
unfairly: "See, God will kill me; I have no hope; but I will
defend my ways to his face" (Job 13:15). In effect, God
has broken the "law" of retributive justice that stands at
the heart of wisdom's ability to maintain social order.
Until Job, wisdom could promise material reward and success for good behavior, and punishment for bad. With Job
that whole structure is called into question:

> Look at me, and be appalled. . . . Why do the wicked
> live on, reach old age, and grow mighty in
> power? . . . The wicked are spared in the day of
> calamity, and are rescued in the day of
> wrath. . . . How then will you comfort me with
> empty nothings? There is nothing left of your
> answers but falsehood. (Job 21:5, 7, 30, 34)

One of the most poignant elements in the book of Job is his recurring lament that his future is cut off, and as a corollary, his hope is gone. His lament parallels very closely the quest for fullness of life that brought us into this wisdom literature. How shall we have a future, when we have no hope in God? Whereas Proverbs promises that "if you find wisdom, you will find a future, and your hope will not be cut off" (24:14), Job laments that God has "uprooted my hope like a tree" (19:10). When God is capricious and wrathful, acting without reason against humans, then life is precarious and uncertain. When there is no continuity, no cohesion, no meaning in life itself, then our spirits are broken.

The book of Job is an excellent example of wisdom's intention to provoke questions, to encourage doubt, to invite testing of experience, to address vital questions. The great power of the book is not that it has definitive answers, but that it trusts the importance of questions. Indeed, many commentators observe that there is no clear solution to the question posed so powerfully by the book. Yet we are told Job is satisfied. What is the source of Job's hope? Perhaps it can be located in the fact that at last God comes to speak with Job—God cares enough to address Job's lament personally. Hope and transformation emerges from the fact of relationship, from the intimacy between the infinite God and the finite man.

Job points us toward exactly that problem which confronts us today: we are too sure either that our faith tradition knows all the answers, or alternatively, too sure it knows none. In Job's day, the older tradition of wisdom represented by Proverbs had lost its momentum, its explanatory power. As noted above, the language of meaning used in Proverbs rested in the elementary concept of retributive justice: you deserve what you get. But as human society became more complex, attentiveness to God's actual presence in life experience waned, and people began to formalize older notions, rather than continue their own search for meaning within paradox. Notions about God became rigid, while social relations became more fluid. In the book of Job, God reminds Job that all notions of the divine are intended only for provisional use; God is greater than anything we can imagine. We are welcome to imagine about the divine, but not to make idols of our imaginings, for God is always more.

27

From our current vantage point, we could observe that a morality based on pain and pleasure is very elementary indeed. Even as individuals, our moral growth evolves from simple pain/pleasure toward conformance to social norms and finally toward principles of justice and compassion.[3] It is hardly surprising that the wisdom tradition itself would outgrow its first stage of moral insight. Simple and direct notions of cause and effect were no longer considered reliable ways to think about the physical world, much less about its moral and spiritual dimensions. In human development there is a natural movement toward a more adequate and comprehensive understanding of connectivity, in which the one seeking explanations becomes a significant participant in the actual flow of events. The very meaning of the idea of God itself is that God is always beyond our current capacity to comprehend, inviting us further into the delights of a fundamentally mysterious universe. So, far from being dismayed by the anguished questions of the book of Job, we can be heartened by the fact that they represent the natural growth of a vital tradition of genuine wisdom.

In the last of the three principal wisdom books, written in the late third century B.C.E., Ecclesiastes questions the whole wisdom enterprise: is it actually possible to discover how to live well? What is the point of careful study of events and consequences in light of the sudden catastrophe that shatters our puny knowledge? Ecclesiastes laments that all human undertaking is vanity, a mere mockery of genuine wisdom, and suggests that the human intellect is incapable of finding meaning in life. The doubts of Job and Ecclesiastes have a remarkably modern ring, for they reveal our own anxieties. Despite all our scientific and technological advancement, what do we really understand? For all our apparent progress, what have we really accomplished? Have we been able to create for ourselves one iota more of genuine happiness or peace? Have we moved one inch closer to discovering how to satisfy our spiritual passions or bring about true justice among people? Why are we still plagued by an inner desire whose persistence reminds us that we have not yet found our true identity?

28

We tend to consult the wisdom tradition whenever serious challenges confront the great story of salvation history, which is the Bible's primary focus. During the dramatic moments of God's rescue of the beloved people (such as the escape from Egypt), the biblical theme of God's saving actions in human history takes the fore. But when the people are being scattered and dispersed, when the prophets' warnings that God is punishing the people for their failure to honor him ring false because, like Job, the Hebrews know their faithfulness, then the sages become important to the people of God. The sages are more at home with the common events of every day than with concepts and abstractions, so they do not give up the quest for meaning in human life even when troubled by suffering or baffled by ambiguity. The sages are curious about what "works" in specific situations: how actions contribute—or not—to ongoing growth in wholeness for the individual and the community. The wise observe how God can be found in routine business transactions or family relationships, those habitual choices that lead either toward more abundant life or to a drying up of vitality.

✆ The Importance of Desire

In the wisdom tradition the wise believe desire can be trusted, because, as God's gift, it teaches them about the real nature of human beings and the world. At the core of wisdom lies a remarkable insight: we know that abundant life exists primarily because its absence haunts us; we *desire* something just out of reach that will not let us rest until we experience it. The Bible begins by explaining not only how things came into existence, but also about how something was "lost." The garden of Eden is an effort to describe a wholeness we once knew. It is this experience of partialness, this ever-present desire for fullness of life, which wisdom claims as a pointer toward the divine reality. Wisdom claims there *is* something more, and the purpose of human life is to seek the More and find rest there. We *know* there is more, because the desire in our hearts was planted there by the Creator, and we can trust that desire.

The importance of desire cannot be overemphasized as a means to fullness of life. Desire's purpose is not so much to bring us to satisfaction, as to deepen our passion. Every time we reach out to God in need, God's response fills not only our present capacity, but also hollows out (or expands) an even greater capacity within us to receive "more" of God (and of ourselves) later. For example, suppose that a man is troubled by his apparent inability to be kind to his mother-in-law; every time he speaks with her, he finds himself unintentionally putting her down. Turning to God for help, this man genuinely seeks to be more gracious to this woman who is such a fixture in his life. Say that after six months of prayer and practice, he finds that he is genuinely enjoying her company—and that he also has a deepened capacity in himself to love his wife more. Desire is not dissimilar to a tiny fetus gradually enlarging the interior space in which it dwells, to accommodate not only its own growing size but also to create

29

the necessary space for new birth. We are meant to pay attention to our desire as a pointer leading us toward what God has in mind for us, toward fullness of life.

In the words of a poem,

> Desire carves out capacity to shelter the unknown,
> to welcome mystery
> To fall on knees before the One the heart has
> always longed for.[4]

30

Our deep longing for life is the means God uses to form our essential being, shaping us to share in the ongoing creation of the world. Human wisdom is intimately linked with human desire. Throughout the wisdom writings we find the language of urgency that can be associated with the building up of desire.

> Let your heart hold fast my words.... Get wisdom; get insight: do not forget, nor turn away from the words of my mouth. Do not forsake her, and she will keep you; love her, and she will guard you. (Proverbs 4:4-6)

> Set your desire on my words; long for them, and you will be instructed. Wisdom is radiant and unfading, and she is easily discerned by those who love her, and is found by those who seek her. She hastens to make herself known to those who desire her. (Wisdom 6:11-13)

> To fear the Lord is fullness of wisdom; she inebriates mortals with her fruits; she fills their whole house with desirable goods.... She heighten[s] the glory of those who [hold] her fast. (Sirach 1:16-19)

Wisdom is often referred to as female, and usually called by the feminine Greek name Sophia, which means wisdom. Indeed, the words for wisdom in Hebrew and

Latin are also feminine nouns. The many reasons why this aspect of the Divine Being is so consistently understood as feminine are grist for another book, but here we can surely note the truth of God's great attractiveness to us, arousing in us a desire for something like conjugal union. Only the wise among us dare to risk the plunge into the wholehearted embrace of God. God is not only Truth, but also Love and Beauty beyond all other, a beauty designed to delight us, a love designed to seduce us with the strength of our desire for Life itself. Our erotic urges are mimicries of the foundational pull toward intimacy with God's very self. Oddly, such language sounds almost offensive to our sexually provocative modern culture, whereas it has a long and honored tradition in Christian literature. Wisdom teaches that desire is a reliable inner attraction toward the most profound truths of our being and our relationships. But we moderns cannot quite figure out how to connect with our longings at a trustworthy level.

31

Obviously we need discernment in the exercise of desire. Suppose we follow every impulse that attracts us, like a puppy dog trotting after every pair of legs it encounters. Soon we will be exhausted by running back and forth, never focused on anything. Or suppose we sit down at our computer and order everything we find on the Internet that beckons to us. Soon we will have a mound of credit card debt that will take years to repay. If we allow the first hints of desire to carry us off willy-nilly, we are unlikely to find fullness of life. We find only fragmentation, the desire to acquire and possess taught by consumerism, the constant yearning for more things. In contrast, the desire God implants in our being is one intended to unify us, to gather all our life around a coherent core. Some of our superficial desires can be recognized as impulses whose satisfaction would cause distress for others; at this level desires are obviously not life-bringing. One of the best ways to invite our earliest impulses of desire to deepen toward more reliable levels is to ask ourselves over and over again what we truly desire, allowing each response to move further toward foundational motives. Jesus' question to the disciples in John 1:38 ("What are you looking for?") reminds us that God invites us to articulate what we desire, in order that *we* know what we truly seek from God.

The serious work of attending to desire as spiritually reliable is difficult in our culture, which profoundly distrusts desire as a guide to spiritual maturity. One important reason for such distrust is the way desire is manipulated and multiplied in contemporary advertising. Another factor heightening our distrust of desire is the (mistaken) belief that psychology reveals in every person a dark subconscious shadow that is antagonistic to our best impulses. Too often we suspect ourselves to be wild and lawless in our inmost being, and decide that constant discipline is necessary to overcome these antisocial and unholy tendencies. Such pop psychological shorthand is fed by confused religious language about our human sinfulness as if it were stronger than the mercy and love of God. All this contributes to our impulse to fill up our emptiness by consuming even more. We think of desire as hunger for a *known* thing, which will be satisfied by the possession of that thing; we interpret it as a sign of dissatisfaction, a need that should not be left unmet.

Such a view of desire, although prevalent, rests on a distortion both of religious wisdom and psychological insight. Good psychology understands and encourages people to dig below the obvious desire to uncover the more authentic human desires for love, self-esteem, and competence. And, as we have seen, the ancient wisdom of many religious traditions supports desire as the way God leads us to life itself.

Theologian Sebastian Moore has observed that the desire beneath all others is the desire for God. We *want*

32

God to exist. Modern thought has tended to view our desire for God as proof that God is only an illusion we create for our comfort, but this idea inverts the best of centuries of Christian thought. Moore asserts that "the desire for there to be God springs not from our weakness but from our strength, not from a sense of worthlessness but from a passionate sense of our worth."[5] We desire to be someone beyond our own limits: in effect, to transcend ourselves. And desire is the *only* thing that can lead us further than imagination can carry us. Self-discipline, no matter how stringent, cannot lift us beyond what we know. Rules and laws, no matter how severely enforced, cannot enlarge our hearts. Only desire opens us to the touch of another in a way that alters our very being. Only love brings us into a state of willingness to be changed beyond our controlling. Strangely enough, real desire is longing for something that does not so much *satisfy* us as *expands our capacity* for satisfaction.

Consider the powerful argument made in the fourth century by bishop Gregory of Nyssa (brother of Benedict's mentor, Basil) in a book called *The Life of Moses*. Gregory claims that the secret of the spiritual life rests in a continual heightening of our desire for the good. Gregory was perplexed by the curious account in Exodus 33, in which Moses presses Yahweh to reveal himself, but the Lord responds that Moses may see only his back. Praying over this passage, Gregory concludes that the soul is made to desire, and to keep desiring, always "straining forward to what lies ahead" (Philippians 3:13). In other words, God satisfies our desiring in such a way as to increase our capacity; the filling of our desire dilates our hearts so that they are able to receive even more.

Thus from the spiritual point of view, the goal of desire is to deepen our desire. If desire in us is a capacity for God's abiding presence, then it is always too small. Desire is more like a mystery than a puzzle. With desire, as with

33

mystery, the process is one of reaching an immediate horizon, only to discover that the horizon has broadened out ahead, inviting us further up and further in. With a puzzle, the process is one of finding an answer or solution and stopping there. At first, we may be dismayed by the realization that, just as we cannot control mystery, we will never fully satisfy desire, at least in this life. But as we play with the process a bit, we discover the exciting wonder that there is always more to challenge and engage us, always more to draw us deeply into the mystery that is at the heart of life.

A modern Christian apologist, C. S. Lewis, emphasized the importance of strengthening desire as an aide to spiritual development. In his marvelous capacity for metaphor, Lewis invites us to think of a raft in the ocean, lost and adrift, carrying several people. The fact that those people are hungry and thirsty does not mean that they will be fed. But it does mean that they are beings who are nurtured by food and drink, and that they inhabit a world where such nourishment exists. Lewis admonishes us that we do not desire too much, but too little: "We are fooling about with drink and sex and ambition when infinite joy is offered us."[6] We have let our desires be limited by our puny imaginations, rather than allowing them to catch us up to the divine.

ॐ Experience as a Source of Wisdom

Wisdom's core insight is this: we know that abundant life exists primarily because its absence haunts us. We *desire* something just out of reach that will not let us rest until we experience it. The tradition of wisdom shows the value of desire, and further exploration reveals that genuine human desire is a powerful key by which we can not only access the older tradition, but also begin to unlock the divine within our own contemporary experience. What then are the means by which we can begin to see, respond, and shape the contours of our daily life around this insight?

Recall that wisdom's approach is always concrete and specific, looking to actual daily experience for information about how things are. Wisdom's approach is to gather data from careful observation, only then drawing conclusions. Using actual experience of life as its starting point marks wisdom's approach to the whole, holy life, especially in contrast with other familiar modes of religious thought. These set forth certain universal principles, understood to be received though revelation, as the cognitive boundary within which life with God is to be understood. Instead, wisdom wants to examine life experience to discover or uncover the traces of God there. The focus on life events gives every single person access to insight, to clues about fullness of life, to the heart of God. Reflection on life events is a powerful way to be liberated from the limitations of commonly accepted cultural perspectives that are no longer helpful or meaningful.

Our ideas about God tend to become rigid when we are buffeted by change, so wisdom's search through experience is a way to renew the relevance and explanatory power of traditional core values. For wisdom is not limited to credal formulations, but instead reaches into daily events, reflecting upon them and seeking to reveal their treasures. In time, the sages often make their way back to foundational beliefs, but in the process they have found new language or different perspectives to help illumine the old ways of thought. That is why the people of God have sought wisdom especially in times of confusion and disruption: when the old generalizations would not hold, how could they make sense of their lives?

The simple answer of wisdom is, look afresh! Pay attention. Watch what is occurring before your eyes and ears, and reflect on what you have seen. In times of great cultural change, obsolete or limiting perspectives can often be reconceived by looking at actual experience with fresh eyes. If something is genuinely true of human life, the sages argue, we will be able to discover it within the events and circumstances we encounter daily. The only requirement is that our own perspective be as fresh as the data we scrutinize. In order for experience to reveal the truth, we must be radically open and receptive to being changed by our encounter with that experience.

36

However, experience, especially as we make sense of it, is more elusive and variable than we might imagine. We only experience what we notice, and we only notice what we have been taught to see. One example is the more than twenty words in the Eskimo language for snow, which would be meaningless to an outsider who had not learned how to observe the nuances of snow: icy in contrast to wet, banked in contrast to blowing, and so forth. By comparison, in the misty highlands of Scotland many words for rain punctuate the language: it is unlikely that those from sunnier climates would be sensitive to the hybrid of mist and fog referred to by the Scottish word *har*.

Human beings cannot be simultaneously aware of every single stimulus in every single moment. We perceive the world selectively, tending to notice that which is familiar or important to us. Let's imagine three people are looking at an automobile. A potential purchaser might focus primarily on the make, model, and color of the car, while a repair professional might observe a dented fender and several scratches in the paint. The third person might be much more aware of the radically new hairstyles on the occupants of the car. While each of the three is theoretically able to see all that the others do, the third person might not even be aware of the model of the car, even when it was pointed out. So what we perceive is largely confined to what we expect to perceive. And our expectations are generally shaped by our interests and training.

Occasionally, phenomena that are strange or unusual to us will slip through our awareness, especially when we are silent and alone, but we may or may not register them, depending on how receptive we are to the unexpected. Often we discount such unusual phenomena as "only my imagination." We tend to think that "facts" are gathered primarily by information equally available to all inquirers regardless of their capacity to "see." We want to know whether or not a specific observation is "real," whether it "really" happened. If the event occurs outside the range of the "normal," we often judge it to be mere illusion. Is a rainbow only a trick of perspective? Did God touch my life in that deep assurance that all would be well, or did I only imagine the comfort I needed? When we risk acknowledging as real those experiences outside the acceptable framework of consensus, we may find that those experiences change us.

It seems easy to seek fullness of life when we are drawn by the delightful glimpses of desire. But when desire carries us toward new and unsettling encounters, we may feel that we have entered a whirlwind with no guideposts in sight. We may feel even more adrift and uncertain than we did before, not unlike Ecclesiastes' conviction that "all is vanity." We lose control of outcomes, no longer have a reliable sense of what is cause and what is effect, and become radically subject to powerful movements beyond our understanding.

We all have an interest in maintaining our existing worldview intact; after all, it is the overall perspective or framework from which we observe and interpret experience. A known and accepted worldview offers apparent and necessary stability as we interact with each other and the world, giving both personal and social or cultural security. In order to observe actual experience with fresh eyes, we must be open to possible changes in these foundational ways of thinking. Such change is the psychological and social equivalent of an earthquke: the very ground on which we counted is suddenly unstable. No one *wants* to embark upon such a distressing task, however meaningful we hope it might be.

In recent decades scholars have discovered patterns suggesting that the primary method of human development is precisely through the disruption and subsequent restructuring of frameworks of understanding. Educators first saw this pattern of development in the learning process of children.[7] A child at the earliest level of awareness passes through the disorienting discovery that her old categories of understanding no longer work. When too many new bits of information render those old categories insufficient, she will suddenly seem to break through into a more adequate perceptual framework.

This mental/emotional process through which the child passes can be understood through an analogy. Imagine a child's playhouse, quite large enough for a boy to play inside. Inside there are several regular rooms, each with a number of cubbyholes and nooks and crannies along the walls and a number of boxes on the floor. Each of these openings or containers is labeled for certain categories of data, and the arrangement, size, and labeling of the boxes represent the child's existing view of the world. Whenever anything happens, the boy makes a sign describing the event, and carefully places it within an opening. We can readily imagine that not only do the openings begin to get quite full, but as he grows older he experiences events that will not fit *any* of his categories of data. These new events are of a type not seen before, they are a strange size, or he has too many of one kind and too few of another. Finally, the pile of loose and unclassified signs grows so unwieldy that the whole playhouse structure becomes unbalanced. And at last the entire structure collapses, much to his dismay. All of his life is represented in those random symbols, and they are now without a home. He has lost his framework; his existing "worldview" is altogether gone. But how else could he begin to build a new and more roomy hideout, far more adequate for his maturing range of experience?

In the case of the child's physical and psychic development, it is not difficult to see that a period of disequilibrium may be a necessary condition for movement toward a more comprehensive and mature stage of growth. We feel confident that there is a natural progression from one stage of maturity to another, and we are comfortable in assuring children that the discomfort of the moment will pass in a process that is benevolent.

39

But it is another thing altogether to realize that adults go through the *same* developmental process. The work of developmental psychologists such as James Fowler points toward the continuation of movement through significant developmental stages in adult life, especially in the areas of moral and spiritual growth. The movement from one stage to another reveals the same dynamics in adults as in children: there must be a period of disruption and apparent "chaos" in the evolution to a deeper level of maturity. Furthermore, the same stability/disruption/reintegration process happens not only in individual adult development, but also in our life in common. The contemporary interest in major paradigm shifts is an expression of this growing awareness.

Yet such work is always experienced as dangerous and risky. If the perspectives and values that have served us well in the past now appear to be inadequate or even seem to be crumbling—dare we risk that another and more "mature" form of values will emerge? In the analogy of the boy's playhouse, we see how destruction is necessary in the period of disequilibrium. Perhaps we can endure that loss, but what assurance do we have that a new and better setting will emerge? When the disruption seems to involve large segments of our social and cultural environment, often in a painful and violent catharsis, how do we know that the destruction will lead to new life?

The answer is, we do not. Nothing is certain, and it can sometimes seem that the destruction is more powerful than any inklings of new life. Life in its beginnings is always vulnerable, whether it is the tiny green bud on a cherry tree or an infant laid in swaddling cloths in a manger. But as the latter image suggests, the assurance of the gospel of Christ is precisely that God's very self dwells in such vulnerable beginnings, collaborating with us to bring forth ultimate resurrection. As those committed to the path of Christian spiritual development, we would be glad to participate in the stormy transition from death to life, if only we could be certain that is what is happening. But we are never certain.

As a result, many of us choose not to leave our familiar old playhouses, no matter how cramped they become. We try to refuse disturbing new data. We deny even direct messages, refusing to accept events that we cannot mentally or emotionally manage. We carefully limit our experience and narrow our perceptions, hoping to avoid indefinitely facing the truth that our worldview is no longer adequate. Many inviting distractions seem to offer escape from the reality of our situation—television, movies, the Internet and its virtual reality. We can live vicariously, fill ourselves with pills or alcohol, be frantically busy. It is all too easy to opt out, to avoid and refuse the opportunities for growth by fearful clinging to a nearly collapsed worldview.

Two strong motives can help us risk an openness to God's invitation into the unknown. One of these is discomfort and disturbance. We have seen how the collapse of an old worldview in effect forces us to confront change. When careful walls against reality lie in shambles around our feet, we are unalterably confronted with life as it really is. Such unavoidable disturbances may take the form of a heart attack or cancer diagnosis, or the loss of an apparently secure job, or an adult child's revelation of his or her homosexuality. In such times we are forced to confront our mortality, our inability to control the lives of others, the inescapable contingency of our own lives. We find ourselves living in the ruins of carefully contained lives, confronted with the invitation to surrender to God's healing presence and experience newness of life within apparent chaos. Not everyone will embrace such possibilities for growth, but the presence of others who know God's promises and have experienced God's resurrection in their own lives can be a tremendous support at such a time.

41

The other powerful motivator helping us to risk change is desire. We have seen how central the role of desire is in spiritual maturity. But perhaps we have not yet realized that desire is the strongest possible incentive to reach out beyond the known into the ambiguous unknown. We may imagine that God's primary means of motivating us to choose fullness of life is to punish us when we fail to choose rightly. But a far stronger incentive for action is the longing of a person in love. For the sake of the beloved, whether my child or my spouse or my best friend, I will transcend myself again and again. When the beloved is God's very self, nothing can restrain me from the perilous leap into the unknown, for I intuitively sense that I will find there something infinitely more wonderful than anything I have yet known.

It requires great courage to give ourselves over to the uncertainties of experience within God's very life, and we will still likely feel we are caught in the whirlwind for a time. Such radically new experience may even seem to disrupt what we think we know about God. But the sages approach experience in the confidence that the created world finds its meaning within the purposes of God. Wisdom integrates the foundational power of desire in its approach to experience. Our shared past as a people of

God reveals God's intention for us as co-creators of history. Our present experience is fully capable of leading us toward a promising future, when we have learned to attend and respond to the deepest desire of our being contained within the nurturing purposes of the Holy One. In the union of experience and desire, God's presence is directly received in every time and place.

42

Benedictine scholar Aquinata Bockmann points out that the English word "experience" is formed from the Latin, *ex* and *per-ire,* meaning an event that takes one out of oneself. It contains an element of the unexpected, something that can happen *to* us, such as death. It involves movement—going out, over oneself, to God. For Christian spiritual writers, experience is entering into the mystery of God, God who moves toward us and in us, who surprises and encounters us.[8] With this definition, we can see that desire is the escort leading us into experience, as a way of opening our limited perspective toward the greater vision of God's very self. When we give ourselves to that larger vision and presence, new possibilities emerge in and for us.

This view of wisdom as discovered in life events and motivated by desire was taken up by Benedict of Nursia, as he combined experience and faith, holding up one and then the other to expand the heart's capacity for God's continuing surprises. Benedict set his whole Rule in the context of the question of how to live the abundant life, the life for which we were made, even and especially when that seems most difficult. Fortunately for us, Benedict does not just state the theory, but like other sages he endeavors to show how the theory can be lived in daily practice. While Benedict wrote his Rule for his own sixth-century community, it continues to offer fresh springs for monastics and others living today. Let us now turn to Benedict's insights in the Rule, especially in the Prologue, to help us translate wisdom into our own nurturance of life.

CHAPTER 2

Benedict and Wisdom

The older and wise can console and comfort....
(RB 27:2-3, paraphrased)

B enedict's Rule adopted the framework of the wisdom
tradition with primary attention to the way daily
experience—the active or practical life—could reveal
God's presence. Community life is valued both as a repository of wisdom's values and as a means of passing them
along. The Rule emphasizes daily life as the primary place
of spiritual learning and experience. Most of the Rule is
concerned with ordering such elements of life as meals and
farming and crafts and relationships, seeing every aspect
as an opportunity to practice life in abundance. That practice is aimed at two goals: purity of heart and love of God.
Purity of heart means the simplicity and singleness of
intention found by turning from evil and doing good.
Love of God is understood above all as gift, the gift of

overflowing charity given by the Spirit when our hearts are free for it.

If we seek a specific section of the Rule that reveals wisdom's insights, we can do no better than the Prologue, the first fifty verses setting out the purpose and method of the Rule. Let us follow the Prologue verse by verse to see how it directs our search for fullness of life.

44

∽

> Listen, O my son, to the precepts of the master, and incline the ear of your heart: willingly receive and faithfully fulfill the admonition of your loving father; that you may return by the labor of obedience to him from whom you had departed through the laziness of disobedience.

The introductory phrase "Listen...and incline the ear of your heart" parallels the key phrase in scripture indicating that what follows will be wise counsel. Listen means pay attention, watch, be alert: something important is going on. The mind is not being addressed with mere information; instead the heart is sought, as the human contemplative organ, the most sensitively attuned receptor for transformative encounter with God. "Receive the admonition of your loving father" has a deliberately double meaning: the father or parent is the one charged with responsibility for teaching children how to live, and in this case means the abbot as the surrogate parent. But it also means more than the human parent; the word play suggests that the true parent is the divine Creator, to whom we owe our being and from whom we receive all that is necessary for true life. It is characteristic of human life that we all forget. It is hard to remember from day to day whence we come and what we are truly about. We are "disobedient" when we neglect to watch and pay attention to what is genuinely important. The lesson we will learn here is how to remain "obedient," that is, listening for the life that is truly ours.

45

To you therefore, my words are now addressed, whoever you are, that through renouncing your own will you may fight for the Lord Christ, the true king, by taking up the strong and bright weapons of obedience.

A few verses later, the Prologue returns to the first person plural (we) that it generally maintains throughout. But Benedict could not resist putting these first few verses of the Rule in direct address to each one of us. "You, listen! It is not some imaginary other, but you, yourself to whom I am (God is) speaking." Stop reading now, take a deep breath, and realize that whatever is going on here involves you directly. This is for you, whoever you are.

The next words have the bracing shock of a dash of cold water. "Renounce your own will in order to fight for your king." We may well find ourselves repelled by this image: "Fighting and violence only add to problems, they do not solve them. Besides, I'm struggling to trust myself, not renounce my own will in obedience to someone else." We are entitled to disagree with the text if we choose, but the foundational principle of gathering wisdom from another place and period is to start by giving the text the benefit of the doubt. What is Benedict intending to say that might be helpful to us? Can we tease something fruitful out of this passage? Benedict saw aggressive impulses as healthy, so long as they were turned against whatever threatens to separate us from a sense of wholeness in God. Most of us have occasional thoughts of unworthiness, denying the love of others because we feel we do not deserve it. Such thoughts are rightly fought as mere temptations to isolate us from God, and we need strong and bright weapons to overcome their power. The will that must be renounced is *willfulness,* the arrogant assumption that we are self-contained and self-sufficient; the will we must embrace is *willingness,* the receptivity and flexibility to be shaped by God's loving care.

46

∽

First, whenever you begin any good work, beg of him with most earnest prayer to perfect it; so that he who has now granted us the dignity of being counted among the number of his sons may not at any time be grieved by our evil deeds. For we must always so serve him with the good things he has given us that not only may he never, as an angry father, disinherit his children; but may never as a dread Lord, incensed by our sins, deliver us to everlasting punishment as most wicked servants who would not follow him to glory.

What a wonderful reminder that it is well to begin every activity with a prayer for help in its accomplishment! So often we forget to pray until things go wrong. And how much anxiety is relieved by realizing at the beginning that only work that is a cooperative effort with the Spirit can flourish. We are given many good things; let us express our thanks by enjoying and valuing those. God regards us as his own, and it matters very much how we think and act. We can disappoint and grieve God; and we will certainly reap the natural consequences of our behavior, for good or ill.

> Let us then at last arise, since the Scripture arouses us saying: it is now time for us to rise from sleep. And let us open our eyes to the deifying light; let us attune our ears to what the divine voice admonishes us, daily crying out: Today if you hear his voice, harden not your hearts. And again, You who have ears to hear, hear what the Spirit says to the churches.

The continuous and urgent word of wisdom is, "Wake up!" Do not pass through the days of your life without noticing. The verbs here are strong ones: rise, open, cry out, hear! Do not let your senses be dulled to the wonder that surrounds you. How can you expect fullness of life if you are not present to the "now"? The phrase "harden not your hearts" is taken from Psalm 95, where it refers to Exodus 17:7. The Israelites hardened their hearts in the wilderness because they did not believe that God was with them. God had worked a great miracle on their behalf at the Red Sea only a few months before, but in the tiring march through the desert they forgot. We too forget that God is with us. But each day, each moment, is a new opportunity to remember.

> And what does [the Spirit] say? Come, my sons, listen to me, I will teach you the fear of the Lord. Run while you have the light of life, lest the darkness of death seize hold of you.

"Listen, my child, to what I will say." We cannot be reminded too often that there is wisdom to be gained for those who will listen. We have been given fullness of life; to keep it we must choose it. A fundamental tenet of wisdom is that it begins with the fear of the Lord. This phrase is found throughout the wisdom literature (as in Psalm 112:1 and Proverbs 1:7), and its meaning is of the sort we discussed earlier: the phrase cannot really be understood until our hearts are large enough to receive its fullness. At first it may simply mean that we will be punished if we do not obey, for the earliest stage of moral development is simple obedience to pain and pleasure. But as we live wisely, we become aware of a desire for union and harmony with God. To be without this relationship becomes inconceivable, and we will do nothing to risk its loss.

48

And the Lord, seeking his own workman in the multitude of the people to whom he cries out, says again, Who is it who desires life, and longs to see good days? (Psalm 34:12) And if you, hearing him, respond, "I am the one!" God says to you: If you desire true and everlasting life, keep your tongue from evil and your lips from speaking deceit. Turn aside from evil and do good; seek peace and pursue it. (Psalm 34:13-14)

These verses contain our key wisdom question: do you desire life? This desire is a longing, and it is a longing for something *now*. We want to see good days. In the words of another psalm, we want to "see the goodness of the LORD in the land of the living" (27:13). This is not so much a desire for *eternal* life or immortality as it is a desire that the days of our lives be full of an unimaginable sweetness and joy. And Benedict directs this longing just as Psalm 34 does, just as the wisdom tradition always does, to those daily habits by which we conduct our lives. Don't lie. Avoid evil. Do good. Seek peace. The sublime longing finds its fulfillment in a particular way of being in the world.

And when you have done these things, my eyes will be upon you, and my ears towards your prayers; and before you call upon me, I will say to you, "Behold, I am here." What can be sweeter to us than this voice of the Lord inviting us, dear brothers? Behold in his loving kindness the Lord shows us the way of life.

Not only we ourselves desire life in abundance; God desires it for us as well. Not only must our eyes and ears be attentive; God's "eyes" and "ears" are always attentive to us. Benedict's vision of the prophet Isaiah is such a comforting one: he evokes for us not so much the young Isaiah, calling out to God that he is here to serve God (6:8) as the later Isaiah, who himself hears God's reminder that God's very self is here to serve us (58:9). God does not wait for us to puzzle out the way of life; God rushes in before the soul finishes its prayer to show us the way. And the way is to rejoice in this constant, loving Presence.

Having therefore girded our loins with faith and the performance of good works, with the Gospel as guide, let us walk in his paths, that we may deserve to see him who has called us into his kingdom. Is the tent of this kingdom where we wish to dwell? Unless by our good deeds we run there, we shall never arrive there. But let us with the Prophet

inquire of the Lord, saying to him: "Lord, who shall
dwell in your tent, or who shall rest upon your holy
mountain?" (Psalm 15:1)

God has called each of us and offered to walk with us
along the path of life. What follows is not only a journey
but also a place of rest, a tent where we find our dwelling.
Our part is to be ready—ready through our willingness
to receive and through the good deeds we practice.
Sometimes the idea of resting and dwelling is more comforting than the idea of constant journey. The Bible contains both these images—of journey and of home—but the
language of our times seems more comfortable with images
of being "on the go." Dare we rest? Is this indeed where we
wish to dwell? Again, we must decide. But if we *do* choose
to take up our dwelling with God, what are the conditions?
What is required of us?

50

After this question, brothers, let us hear the Lord
responding, showing us the way to his tent, saying:
One who walks without stain and works justice;
one who speaks truth in his heart, who has not
practiced deceit with his tongue; one who has done
no evil to his neighbor, and has not believed false
accusations against his neighbor; one who has
expelled the malignant devil together with all his
advice and persuasiveness out of the sight of his
heart, casting him to naught; and has grasped his
infantile thoughts and hurled them against Christ.

Taken together, Psalm 15 and Psalm 34 form the core of
the practical instruction given in the Prologue of the Rule.
Psalm 15 begins with the question that Benedict understands as a paraphrase of our basic concern. "Who may

dwell in your tent?" is another way of asking "How shall I obtain life?" because abundant life is found only in intimate relationship with the One who completes us. And both questions parallel Psalm 34's promise to show us "the fear of the Lord," reminding us that fearing the Lord (v. 9) is closely connected with tasting the sweetness of the Lord (v. 8).

51

What is required of us, then? The answer is given in the terms preferred by wisdom: it is particular and concrete and relevant to the demands of daily life. Be just. Neither lie to others nor to yourself. Neither make up nor believe gossip about others. We cannot live in easy relationship with God if we are on uneasy terms with our neighbors. And this requirement goes deep, a matter of the heart even more than the mind. Every human being experiences the persuasiveness of inner advice that we know would make trouble. The solution is simple, and found again in a psalm (137:9): throw such thoughts down against the rock of Christ, just as soon as they appear. Do not entertain these temptations even briefly, for they are seductive. But do trust Christ's power to convert their negative energy immediately into fertilizer to enrich good soil.

These are they who, fearing the Lord, are not elated over their own good observance; rather, knowing that the good which is in them comes not from themselves but from the Lord, they magnify the Lord who works in them, saying with the Prophet: Not unto us, O Lord, but to your name give the glory. In this way the Apostle Paul imputed nothing of his preaching to himself, but said: By the grace of God I am what I am. (I Cor. 15:10) And again he says, He who glories, let him glory in the Lord. (II Cor. 10:17)

There is good within us; let us not forget. We can be full of love, able to be creative and contribute to the greater good. It is false modesty to deny and ignore such moments, for we are meant to live most of the time in such a state, and we move toward it by paying attention to what fullness feels like. And what does it feel like? Overwhelming gratitude! Can you recall a time when you achieved something you felt you had earned, and for which you deserved all the credit? Contrast that with a time when everything came together perfectly, and you knew that your hard efforts contributed to something much better than you alone could have created.

52

Benedict has selected sayings of St. Paul that express the latter type of experience, for his reflection and ours.

Hence also the Lord says in the Gospel: He who hears these words of mine and does them is like a wise man who built his house upon rock: the floods came, the winds blew and beat upon that house, and it did not fall; because it was founded upon rock. With these admonitions concluded, the Lord is waiting daily for us to respond by our deeds to his holy guidance. Therefore, in order that we may amend our evil ways, the days of our lives have been lengthened as a reprieve, as the Apostle says: Do you not know that the patience of God is leading you to repentance? For the loving Lord says: I do not desire the death of a sinner, but that he should be converted and live.

Again, we are reminded of our rock-firm foundation in Christ. We can trust the sure ground in which we are rooted. We belong to a people who have built well upon a reliable source, not only for themselves but for the future. We are invited to drink deeply from their wisdom, to find its value for us, and accordingly to live well. God empowers what God invites, providing the resources by which we are enabled to respond. There comes a time when reflection must fold into discernment (choose!), and a time when discernment must fold into discipline (practice!). Our God waits upon us, desiring life for us even more than we desire it for ourselves.

53

Therefore, brethren, having asked the Lord who is to dwell in his tent, we have heard his commands to those who are to dwell there: it thus remains for us to complete the duties of those who dwell there. Therefore our hearts and bodies must be prepared to fight in holy obedience to his commands. And for that which is hardly possible to us by nature, let us ask God to supply by the help of his grace. And if we wish to reach eternal life, escaping the pains of hell, then—while there is yet time, while we are still in the flesh and are able to fulfill all these things by this light of life given to us—we must run and perform now what will profit us for all eternity.

Choose and act. No one else can take these steps for us, not even God. We are given many experiences to observe and plenty of time for reflection. But at last we are confronted with the necessity of choice and the inevitability of action. Even if we decide with our minds not to choose or act, we have thereby made a choice and we act by our refusal. Notice that obedience in the sense required here is not primarily something of the mind, but rather involves a prepared heart and a ready body. We choose and act by the way we invest our time and energy every day of our lives, in the flesh. And we live with the consequences.

54

We have, therefore, to establish a school of the Lord's service. In instituting it we hope to establish nothing harsh or oppressive. But if anything is somewhat strictly laid down, according to the dictates of equity and for the amendment of vices or for the preservation of love; do not therefore flee in dismay from the way of salvation, which cannot be other than narrow at the beginning.

In doing we are learning. The daily practice of seeking wisdom within experience, supported by scripture and the disciplines of life together, deepens our capacity to experience life itself. But in order for this learning to occur, in order for our perspectives to be enriched, we must give ourselves to some rules, a form of schooling for our soul. This school is not intended to be harsh or oppressive, but at times it *will* be difficult. We are endeavoring to surpass ourselves, to grow beyond our limitations, and even to reach beyond our imaginations. To practice this work is periodically to be confused and troubled, or to feel unsettled and even pained, to need to confront anger and lust and self-doubt. We have courage for this work because of the lives of others shared with us. We endure in this work in the confidence that our deepest desires can be trusted.

Truly as we advance in this way of life and faith,
our hearts open wide, and we run with unspeakable
sweetness of love on the path of God's commandments, so that, never departing from his guidance,
but persevering in his teaching in the monastery
until death, we may by patience participate in the
passion of Christ; that we may deserve also to be
partakers of his kingdom. Amen.

55

Benedict's school for the Lord's service directs us to
unremitting attentiveness and sustained support of life
together in community. Sound daily habits lead to wisdom. Scripture and tradition are made vital through the
living presence of the Holy Spirit in our midst. The dilat-
ed, wide open heart is our goal, for the more we can
receive from God, the more we experience the fullness of
life for which we are made.

PART TWO

Virtue

CHAPTER 3

Developing Character

The present moment holds infinite riches beyond your wildest dreams if you will only enjoy them to the extent of your faith and love.... The will of God is manifest in each moment, an immense ocean which the heart only fathoms in so far as it over-flows with faith, hope, and love.[1]

If wisdom is centered in the desire for life, then virtue is the training of desire, the ongoing shaping of our hunger for life toward the good. Virtue is an ability we can develop to choose life day by day, when "life" means something more than biological existence. Life is that elusive abundance for which our soul longs. Virtue is the capacity to live and act in accord with our deep human desire for wholeness.

Virtue takes us the next step in our search for wisdom, because it requires that we begin to articulate more specifically what we mean by the good life, the abundant life.

We must have some notion of the optimum potential of human life: what is the best kind of life to lead? Virtue leads us directly into questions about what we "ought" to be, how we are most likely to realize our potential as humans. What sort of persons do we wish to be? Such questions are not abstract and remote but practical ones, answered hundreds of times each day by our decisions.

60

✂ Character and the Good Life

So what do you believe is possible for you? What is the essence of who you are, and what kind of person do you seek to be? Our hope for our own life inevitably rests in a conscious or unconscious vision of what human nature is, and how we are linked to the whole created world and to God. And that vision is influenced by the time and place and culture in which we live. For example, Aristotle thought of the good life as *eudaimonia,* blessedness, which he saw as full participation in the social and political community of the Greek city state. Accordingly, the virtues he valued led to the formation of character contributing to that vision, virtues such as friendship and justice. A different vision animated the early centuries of the Christian church, confronted with implacable opposition from the Roman authorities. For them, the good life was viewed as welcoming death and martyrdom for Christ's sake; their valued virtues were courage and steadfastness in the face of pain and humiliation. What is the good life for us today, in our times?

We have been considering a vision of the good life in the wisdom tradition that might be described as wholeness or holiness, a sense of being able to live fully according to the inherent possibilities of our being as humans. This vision embodies certain assumptions: that we humans, and the whole created world, are in fact created with a certain purpose encoded within us. The inherent purpose in creation is both unique to each individual and interwoven with the purposes of others into a unity embracing all. The optimum expression of the good life involves the integration of self-esteem and self-surrender—self-esteem in that we value the particular incarnation the divine takes in us, and self-surrender in that we surpass our limits and connect with the whole only through a deliberate awareness of our dependence upon God. We fail to take our rightful part in the unfolding of grace when we are overcome by self-disgust. Yet also we fail to achieve our intimate relationships with the Whole and the Holy if we ignore our limitations and depend on self alone.

61

In this vision, virtue is response to the call to wholeness by the Divine Being with whom each of us exists in dynamic relationship our whole life long. If there is no possibility of an overall concept of "goodness" transcending individuals, then the idea of virtue can have no meaning. Virtue depends upon an external referent, something above and beyond individual taste, something greater than individual whim. Virtue depends upon seeing something desirable and out-of-reach, yet risking to move toward such a God, knowing that God will have to move toward us as well if fullness is to be found. As an expression of the intimate relationship between virtue and the Good, the Christian tradition understands virtue as the confluence of both the acquired (self-discipline) and the infused (gifts of grace). This means that the presence of virtue in humans is caused both by our own rhythmic endeavors to develop qualities of moderation (temperance), courage (fortitude), fairness (justice), and discretion (prudence), and also by God's help in contributing resources beyond our own of faith, hope, and love.[2]

Virtue is the means by which we cooperate with God in forming our character for this work of love. Fundamentally, virtue is the development of a character capable of choosing the good, over and over again. Character gives orientation to life, expressing our intentions and motivations, as integrated consciously or unconsciously in our behavior. Virtue is the term describing the method taught by the Judeo-Christian tradition to construct character, or to build a life around deliberate choices for the good implanted by the Creator in our hearts. In these two chapters on virtue the term refers to moral character; in the final chapter the term "ethics" is used to mean the concrete actions and behavior of someone possessing virtue.

62

We sometimes think of virtue is as rigid, rather prudish behavior, something that leads us away from fullness of life rather than toward it. We associate virtue with such things as obedience, law, and duty, and imagine that it is acquired chiefly by acting in certain prescribed ways that deny ourselves pleasure. On the contrary, the Christian tradition sees virtue at the heart of the spiritual life, as the concrete expression of our turning toward God through every choice, and our deepening ability to become aware that "the present moment holds infinite riches," as the contemplative writer de Caussade puts it. Every thought and action moves us either toward fullness of life or away from it. Over time, virtue integrates a number of specific choices into consistent habits of the heart—a deliberately acquired disposition to be and to act in certain ways, which we are calling character.

We also misunderstand virtue if we think it only as a matter of making specific choices. Rather, virtue resides primarily in the accumulated inclinations that guide our way of being in the world, acknowledging that the ability to choose the good effectively requires habitual training of the will. Virtue requires a focus on habits, our almost unconscious tendencies to choose to be and to act according to fixed patterns, and requires that we embark upon gentle but firm disciplines of mind and heart, rooted in the routines of the daily. Such routines and habits are not mere compliance with externally imposed rules and norms, but instead are essential in creating the fundamental dispositions of our heart toward or away from joy. Virtue empowers sacrifice, strengthens patience, enlivens love. Virtue gives us the ability to commit ourselves, to live from a coherent center of being, fully present to each moment. Without virtue, fullness of life is impossible.

63

✄ Overvaluing Results

Given this understanding, we might well wonder why the notion of virtue seems to many like a musty relic of yesteryear, left to collect dust in the attic rather than brought down into the family room. Why does virtue seem such an alien concept to us these days?

In recent generations we have become wary of "absolutes." Any concept that presumes to speak for all times and people is viewed with suspicion, largely because we think such ideas embody the experience only of those privileged persons with the leisure and status and money for advanced education and theoretical speculation. Many of the ideas once thought eternal and immutable excluded the experience of a vast number of people. So-called absolutes have been decisively challenged by the contemporary valuing of each person's own experience as relevant in the search for fullness of life.

However, postmodern thought has so thoroughly rejected absolutes that it actually asserts the impossibility of naming any good or any common goal of human life. Our present culture is dominated by the view that "the good" is indefinable, incapable of proof or disproof, and hence nothing but a personal opinion.[3] The culture's dominant view implicitly envisions "God" as a matter of personal opinion—who and what you believe in is up to you, because it has little or no "real" objective reference. Likewise, our culture thinks of individuals as entirely self-created, without any encoded moral guidelines. In other words, the vision we have been considering—that fullness of life emerges from cooperation with potential or purpose given by the divine—is starkly at odds with the unstated assumptions of contemporary society. Today we do not speak of inherent goals or purposes for human life because such words are treated as having no objective content whatsoever. The only matters that can be comfortably discussed in public are those of utility. It is irrelevant to speak of the purpose of something. Rationally, conversation is limited to "answerable" questions like, "Does this produce the desired result?" We cannot speak together about what we "ought" to do as humans; we can only see what we "want" to do.

64

Years ago, as a college student, I came to admire the elegant coherence of the social theories of Max Weber. Weber has been called the father of modern bureaucracy for his work showing that organizations can be united not only by a charismatic leader (which raises the dangers of demagoguery) and by common beliefs (which raise the potential for hatred of "outsiders"), but also by a rational network of hierarchical relationships in which each unit performs a particular task without being aware of the whole. It was a theory perfectly suited to the industrial age, an age that sought identical results in operations performed time after time, no matter who performed them. Weber's bureaucratic rationality is the ideal pattern for assuring that economic and efficient means can be applied to any purpose. In effect, Weber created the virtue of efficiency, or utility, which could stand on its own with no particular referent to a basic concept of the good.

Like so many of his contemporaries and successors in related fields, Weber basically asserted that the question of ends, or purposes, was not within his purview. Others could deal with choices about goodness and beauty and love, but such matters were beyond the capacity of "science" to handle. The methodology common to all emerging fields of study was basically reductionist: the whole is separated into component parts, each of which is critically analyzed. This method accomplishes great strides in understanding discrete units, but it does not even attempt to understand the whole.

Weber, for example, could teach you how to get results, but you were on your own in selecting goals. Suppose you have designed a portable ashtray that can be closed up to fit neatly in a shirt pocket or purse. You want to produce a large quantity of these ashtrays and market them widely so that every smoker owns at least one of them. Weber's bureaucratic structure could readily convert your goal into an organizational chart, with separate units for production and marketing, each reporting to a superior who channels necessary information to the other branch. But there is no place within the organization to assess whether the increased availability of ashtrays will contribute more overall to health or to disease. That particular determination of value is irrelevant to the question of how to achieve the optimum sales of portable ashtrays. Bureaucratic rationality asks, what is the most efficient way to achieve the desired result? That efficiency in this task may be shorten the life of the smoker is a hidden and unexamined consequence, beyond the purview of the method.

The focus on utility, or results, had a satisfying certainty to it, an elegant simplicity, as well as being highly effective. The question of means could be dealt with by a mere observer; one did not have to become engaged in an ongoing relationship that might bring significant change to the system. Should we be surprised to find that after fifty-plus years, almost no scholars remain who do claim the question of purpose as within their purview?

Today, our common discourse tends to fall back upon the "rational" languages of economics and politics, both of which set high value on action taken for the sake of the results it will produce. Everyone wants to know "the bot-

65

tom line." We are so accustomed to considering matters in this way that it is difficult even to imagine another perspective. Such an environment makes it very difficult to consider virtue in any creative way. For virtue is about character, the inner development of an integrity that has its own standards in relationship to the good it desires. Virtue must be dissociated from outcome, because character is quickly dissolved if its only measure is results.

66

A simple example will demonstrate. A single woman of great integrity was seeking to buy a home, and in the process found a broker who assured her that she had a preapproved loan whenever she found a house. She soon made an offer that was immediately accepted based on the prior loan approval, only to find that the broker required more from her—she had to make a false statement that would ensure approval of the loan. After a night's wakefulness she decided not to perjure herself, knowing full well that she would probably lose the house. Her decision was the expression of virtue rooted in a vision of the good, and clearly not based on obtaining results. As it turned out, she was able to obtain another loan in time to buy the house, but she would have been willing to live with being a renter for some time to come rather than compromise her integrity. She recognized that to make this decision based on results would corrode her soul, but she also knew that her choice sounded foolish to many people.

⊗ Virtue in Christian Tradition

If virtue as it is widely understood and practiced today is not a particularly attractive model for those who would like to consider it seriously as a value, what might help us bridge this gap? As it so often does, Benedict's understanding of the gospel of Christ enters this situation as a fresh perspective, offering some guidelines that can help us reconsider our own situation. Before we turn to the Rule's own direct wisdom, however, which mostly rests in his powerful and challenging chapter seven on humility, we need to understand the context in which Benedict's ideas emerged, which will aid us in understanding his language.

In writing his Rule Benedict depended upon the theology of the people of his day as well as that of the early church. In particular, he read and studied the writings of John Cassian and recommended that all those in his monasteries study them. John Cassian and a friend had traveled extensively throughout the Egyptian Christian desert monastic communities in the fourth century, recording many of the conversations he had there and systematizing their wisdom for life. As he pulled his notes together, Cassian in turn drew heavily upon the thought of Evagrius Ponticus.

67

We owe a great deal to Evagrius, who is today recognized as one of the most important figures in the history of spirituality for his approach to the question of virtue and the good. in the In the late fourth century Evagrius was an archdeacon in Constantinople, thanks to his friendship with the great Cappadocian theologians, Basil the Great, Gregory of Nazianzen, and Gregory of Nyssa. Like his peers, Evagrius had a strong conversion experience that sent him out into the Egyptian desert to meditate and reflect. Early in the fifth century John Cassian used the writings of Evagrius as a framework for transcribing his conversations with desert *abbas* and *ammas* in two works known as the *Institutes* and *Conferences*. These were primary sources for Benedict's reflection and prayer on the abundant life.

What was Evagrius up to, and why did it make such an impact on the Christianity of his time? It is fair to characterize Evagrius's purpose as similar to our own: he deeply desired the greatest fullness of which human life was capable, and consistent with his understanding of the good life, he sought to cooperate with its unfolding. In observing carefully his own behavior and that of others who chose life in the desert, he began to notice patterns. It was not enough to say they loved God and to leave their homes, he discovered, for they brought their old inner realities with them to the new place. Evagrius noticed that everyone who took God seriously had to face certain common issues: moderation in food and drink, sexual activity, and acquiring material goods. Evagrius's insight was to *face* thoughts about these matters directly, looking at their patterns and effects and exploring the most effective ways to counteract the disruption and dismay they caused.

68

We are wrong if we think that the ancients had no adequate understanding of human psychology. We must abandon such a misconception if we to benefit from the work of Evagrius and Cassian. Their grasp of the inner dynamics of the person is quite thorough and contemporary, frequently surpassing that of some modern psychological theories. We may initially find their terminology hard going, but once we understand their language, we cannot fail to find invaluable assistance in our own efforts to choose life.

Until recently, the persistent problem areas identified by Evagrius were usually called the seven deadly sins. However, it may be more helpful to call these persistent human problems "thoughts"; indeed, Evagrius' own term for them is *logismoi,* better translated as disruptive thoughts or obsessive feelings than as sin.[4] The goal of Evagrius's teaching was *apatheia,* meaning freedom from the inner turbulence caused by such thoughts. In other words, when he looked directly at the flow of thoughts inside his mind, Evagrius saw that they often seemed both chaotic and disruptive. It was with him as with St. Paul's account in Romans, "For I do not do what I want, but I do the very thing I hate" (Romans 7:15).

It is often the same for us. I begin thinking about calling a friend I have not seen for some time, only to find a few moments later that I am filled with guilt for memories of saying the wrong thing on our last meeting, for failing to call her since then, and so forth. In other words, I have quickly turned from fond remembrance to self-induced anguish, from care for another to anxiety about my own failures. There are many other ways I could have dealt with this initial stimulus, but when I am not watching carefully, my thoughts can very quickly catch me up in an all-too-familiar maze. They paralyze not only my own intentions, but also the free play of God's Spirit within me. Another way of thinking about virtue is to say that its goal of being attentive to thought patterns leads to the freedom to move toward fullness of life, cooperating with God in genuine peace and charity.

69

The method Evagrius teaches for such freedom is not suppression of thought or passion, but rather redirecting them toward life. He suggests we begin to move toward virtue by first examining those thoughts that interfere with our intention to lead a virtuous life, exploring how those thoughts can be harnessed and redirected. We are to renounce self-will but not to kill it; our method is to train and guide our thoughts to serve our deepest desire for intimacy with God. Evagrius, Cassian, and their heir, Benedict, are consistent in their conviction that *every* human desire, energy, and capacity—since all are given by God—is intended to contribute to human wholeness. It is only when capacities are excessive, defective, or perverted that they interfere with our best interests.

❧ The Eight Troubling Patterns of Thought

Evagrius's principal work of interest to us is called *The Praktikos,* or *The Practical Life,* in which he sets forth one hundred succinct chapters on the ascetic life and enumerates the eight kinds of evil thoughts.[5] This work is picked up by Cassian and presented in his own fashion in the *Institutes of the Cenobitic Life,* and summarized in *Conference V* of Abbot Serapion, "On the Eight Principal

Faults." The list of eight was consolidated into seven by Thomas Aquinas in the thirteenth century, and traditionally were called "the seven deadly sins." The important thing is not so much whether there are seven or eight or three or twelve, as whether they help us understand and redirect our own troubling patterns of inner disturbance. Some of their concerns will not be of much interest to us; some will be right on target. But since these patterns are associated with basic human tendencies, it is well worth considering them all here.

The set of thought patterns includes gluttony, lust, avarice (greed), anger, sadness (depression or dejection), *acedia* (sometimes called sloth, but better as restless despairing), vainglory, and pride. In general, the sequence moves from thoughts presenting lesser dangers to the soul toward the more dangerous. This makes a certain perverse sense, because beginners in the spiritual life are naturally beset with more obvious and superficial disruptions, whereas the spiritually mature must deal with more subtle and deeply rooted matters. On the other hand, there is no particular inevitability here, nor even an implied hierarchy; often the spiritually adept neglect to deal with the obvious and find themselves again struggling with thoughts they imagined to be long ago conquered.

The sequence of thoughts is presented in groupings related to the three major powers of the soul: lust, anger, and intellect. Notice that we do not really have any words in English to express the positive dimensions of two of these powers, although Christian tradition insists all three are given us by God for our good. The first term, the desiring power, roughly corresponds to the imagery associated with "feminine" energy. We can envision the positive quality of "lust" as the capacity to be attracted, to be drawn out from one's self-centeredness toward something desirable; indeed, we have emphasized here the importance of honoring our deep desires.

70

The second term, the refusing power, is connected to "masculine" energy. We can think of the positive qualities of anger as a kind of refusing or rejecting capacity, the capacity to stand firm in our own truth and not be thrown off balance by ebbs and flows that pressure us. In order to say "yes" to what we desire, we must be able to say "no" to less important things that would exhaust our time and energy.

71

The third and final major power of the soul is the "reasoning" power, the intellect. Too often we tend to associate the mind, or reason, with a relatively narrow range of mental activity that excludes human passion and compassion. In Christian tradition the reasoning power is meant positively to refer to that fundamental capacity of the soul for union with God. It is the sum of all those qualities of mind and spirit teaching us that we are made for relationship with the Divine One, that we are incomplete without the joy of that mutuality. Reason includes those means of inner knowing that lead us to awareness of being companioned by God in all times and places. The ancients called reason the "contemplative" power, coming from the root words *con* ("with") and *templum* ("the temple"): wrapped in the presence of the Holy One.

Since all virtue is ultimately expressed in that magnificent and powerful expression of God's essence known as Love, all vices—or troubling thoughts—are considered to be a distortion of our capacity for love. Those thoughts that distort our desiring capacities are considered expressions of excessive love; those that distort our refusing capacities are considered to express defective love. Finally, those that distort our unitive capacities are expressions of perverted love. Let us now look at each of the eight thoughts in turn.

❦ Excessive Love: Gluttony, Lust, and Greed

The first thought pattern that is an expression of excessive love is known as *gluttony*. This pattern usually relates to food and drink, which are pleasurable and necessary to life. As with all these troubling thoughts, the distortion can take either of two extreme forms: obsession with too much or too little. All virtue consists in right relationship with something, and right relationship can be destroyed either by too constant a connection or by severing the relationship in self-chosen isolation. As Cassian notes, "Excesses meet"—too much and too little have more in common with each other than either has with the moderate, or optimum, point.[6]

In our own day, we recognize that obsession with food can take the form of ingesting either more food than the body can handle, or less; anorexia is often a more serious or at least a more immediate danger to the body than being overweight. In the Egyptian desert, gluttony was often manifested as excessive anxiety about one's health, extreme pickiness about what one could or could not eat, or desire for unnecessary variety in food (sometimes said to be Adam and Eve's sin). Even then, it was clearly seen that such obsessions are doubly inappropriate in light of the starving multitudes who would find such fastidiousness unimaginable. Excessive thoughts always take up room in our spirits that is owed to love of God, neighbor, and self.

The second thought pattern is called *lust*. Lust is about sexual or sensual desire, or as Dante wrote, "the unquenchable fire of wanting." Sex shares some qualities with food and drink: it is basically healthy, and certainly necessary for the continuation of the human race, but also inherently pleasurable. As with food and drink, lust can become excessive in the direction of too much or too little; celibacy can be dangerous to the soul if it is gained at the cost of constant fantasizing, self-deception, or use of others. And lust is as dangerous for married persons as it is for those without long-term commitments, for its essence is using others as objects in the service of a drive. Lust can take the form of "women who love too much," whether or not their obsessions include sexual fantasy; it can also apply to anyone who uses sex to express and enforce power and mastery. Whenever we seek to possess or "own" another in relationship, whether it be God, a human being, a creature, or earth itself, we are controlled by lust.

73

The third pattern of thought is *avarice,* or greed. This concerns our relationship with material goods, and it is unrelenting in our culture. Indeed, as ethicist Alasdair MacIntyre notes, the unrestrained desire for things, once considered a vice by Aristotle, has now become the driving force of modern productive work.[7] In an economy like ours, whose health is determined by the levels of production and consumption, it is very difficult to gain the perspective necessary to understand how damaging avarice can be. In the Egyptian desert monks were also troubled by foolish wants and futile planning for an unreal future. They knew how much power daydreams about things could have, and they were wary of undue attachment to any object. And Benedict seeks to assure that his monks do not claim personal ownership even of a writing tablet. What can be so troubling about possessions?

Remember that the three thoughts in this category of excessive love are all distortions of our power to desire. In our world today, even given the serious addictions to food, drink, and sex, there is no doubt that our most crippling obsession is with material goods. We are shamelessly exhorted to believe that our spiritual hunger for fulfillment can be satisfied if only we have "the right things": the name-brand running shoes, the designer scarf, the highest fidelity CD player, the fastest Internet server, the biggest car, the best-programmed microwave, the purest bottled water. Whether we buy goods or not, most of us have become cynical about desire as merely a trap. We may hope that our deep longing for "something more" will be temporarily satisfied with a new purchase; but we really do not believe that desire is capable of leading us to genuine fulfillment because it is so blatantly manipulated in our consumer economy. We long for security and safety, yet fear to relinquish control of our ability to shore up our fragile ego boundaries with possessions. We are stuck in an endless cycle of greed where nothing is ever enough. No other competitor comes close to matching the effectiveness with which greed prevents us from honestly reflecting on our fundamental neediness for God.

✑ Defective Love: Anger, Sadness, and Despair

We turn now to the second group of troublesome thought patterns, those pertaining to our human power of refusing or rejecting. If "desiring" is comparable to our capacity to attract and be attracted, then "refusal" is comparable to our capacity to be firm, or "at one" in ourselves, protective of those things we value. Distortion of this quality shows up in the dissolution of our will, an inability to stand firm for something. As with desiring, distortion here can occur both in the direction of excess or of insufficiency. We can have too little of this firm self-protectiveness or too much. We aim neither to be willful and arbitrary, nor to be limp and passive in the face of injustice. What then are the patterns of thought that display defectiveness of the will?

The first pattern in this category, and the fourth in our overall list of eight thoughts, is *anger*. As lust summarizes the brokenness of our desiring power, so anger summarizes the brokenness of our refusing power. We may find it difficult to see clearly the defects of a God-given power if we have not first begun to name its value and purpose. Overall, the tradition's insight was that these irascible

powers were given in order to help us refuse those distractions that prevent our wholehearted turning toward
God. The special temptation here is to turn our rejecting
powers *against other people* rather than against our own
inner willfulness. For example, if I consistently find it difficult to commit to any relationship of true intimacy, it is
easy to blame flaws in the people I date. If I tend to ver-
bally abuse those around me, it is easier to focus on their
stupidity than to face the truth of my reactive hostility. If
I regularly buy more than I need, I can readily point to the
danger of being caught short in a crisis rather than admit
I am hoarding more than my fair share of basic goods.
Anger and violence often are a spontaneous reaction to
not getting our way, and as such they are defective forms
of our refusing capacity.

75

On the other hand, an equally defective form of this
capacity is never to have any opinion, never to set any firm
personal priorities. When I am in a group deciding to see
a movie, do I say what appeals to me, or always accept the
preferences of others (while resenting that I never get to
see the movies I like)? Do I regularly give up my own quiet
time or nurturing activity in order to meet yet one more
need? Do I speak up and offer help when I notice an injustice being done, or go along with everyone else, carefully
ignoring the situation? When I myself have been treated
unfairly, do I make an opportunity to present my case, or
do I swallow the hurt instead, nursing it inwardly for
years? Whenever fear alone stops me, whether fear of punishment or fear of disapproval, then I must consider
whether I am relinquishing my powers of refusal.

The power to refuse, the power to take a stand and
stand firm, includes not only the energy to initiate strong
action, but also the ability to be patient, to wait, to
endure. Refusal encompasses not only beginnings, but also
persistence, steadiness over the long haul. It is defective
when anger blinds us or encourages self-deception. It fails

when our thoughts circle round and round a festering resentment of the ways people have wronged us. It is dysfunctional when we are busy either justifying ourselves or vilifying ourselves. Our refusal capacity functions optimally when we can entrust ourselves freely and fully to God's mercy and love.

76

The second pattern of thoughts, those characterized by sadness, is often eliminated from contemporary lists of "sins," perhaps because it is difficult for us to imagine how it can be a failure of will or a failure of love. What can sadness have to do with the refusing powers of our soul? Sadness is often described as dejection or depression, or sometimes supplanted by the notion of envy and jealousy, because the two are closely related. But in Evagrius's and Cassian's schema, envy is a subset of the broader category of sadness. Sadness is basically a refusal to accept what is, a refusal of the reality that exists, and as such is a defect in the intended operation of refusal. In the Serenity Prayer attributed to Reinhold Niehbur we can now recognize this aspect of the refusing power of the soul: "God grant me the serenity to accept the things I cannot change, the courage to change the things I can, and the wisdom to know the difference." Sadness is a refusal to accept the things we cannot change, and thus is a refusal to live fully in the present moment.

Maybe we wade in grief for what has been, or for what was lost; perhaps we dwell on the good old days. Sometimes sadness is connected with the need to compare ourselves to others, and the inevitable disappointment that comes when we fall short. Benedictines pray at the time of their consecration that God will not disappoint them in their hope, and this is fundamentally a prayer guiding them in right use of their refusing capacity: to focus their hope on life in God, and not to allow themselves to be distracted by the myriad ways in which they fail. Discernment is required to weave the way between too little and too much. When a major loss has been experienced, we can avoid reality by refusing to grieve at all; but to allow the grief to continue indefinitely is no less a refusal of the ongoing possibilities of life. To use our refusing powers in these ways is to abuse them.

The third pattern of thoughts connected with the refusing power is *acedia,* which is one of those untranslatable words sometimes called "sloth" but better rendered as "restless despairing," or, as it is sometimes known, the "noonday devil." This particular pattern does not usually appear initially, but comes after we have made a good start and established a new rhythm. Then there comes a time when everything seems tasteless. Nothing engages our interest; we feel restless and dissatisfied, bored not only with what is, but with anything we can imagine flowing from what is. We might imagine this kind of thinking to be something like a midlife crisis: we feel weary, wondering if this is all there is, asking why we are doing this. A cloud of discouragement follows us everywhere. Theologian Diogenes Allen suggests that these feelings are associated with a sense of failure; we may or may not have actually failed, but we feel in this moment that our lives are worth nothing at all.[8]

In this thought pattern it is especially easy to see that thoughts also involve feelings, and that feelings often accompany powerful mental distractions from our movement toward God. *Acedia* teaches us to remember that feelings will pass; we may well have them, but we are more than our feelings. At other levels of being than thinking and feeling, we can make choices and stay faithful to those choices. Again, the will—the heart's power to claim God—has the ability to refuse to be swayed by such temporary ebbs and flows. The will can choose God above all and in all, and simply but firmly remain steady on course toward what has been claimed as best for us, what is known to be true and good.

77

As always, the exercise of this power of refusal requires discernment. There are times when feelings are the source of new information that we must attend to and try to understand honestly and fully. But equally there are times when feelings are mere fluctuations in the shape of things; if we refuse to engage them, they simply flow in and out of our awareness. It takes time and practice to recognize when to attend to and when to ignore our feelings.

It may surprise us to realize that the exercise of the irascible capacity seldom involves us in angry, hostile, or war-like confrontation. The essence of this capacity is an inner strength, the ability to stand for our own inner certainty, the ability to persist with joy. Anger, sadness, and despair are all defects in the intended operation of our refusing power; as we practice standing firm against such defects, we begin to discover a quality of inner strength accompanied by peacefulness in serving our God.

✑ Perverted Love: Vainglory and Pride

Finally, we explore the third group of troublesome thought patterns, those relating to our powers of reasoning. Remember that Evagrius and Cassian understood reason as including a much broader scope of activity than the merely logical. For them, reason was above all the ability to know Truth, the human capacity to receive the divine life not just with our minds, but also with our souls. Reason is the power that brings us into ongoing communion with the Holy One, into that relationship necessary for us to become the selves we are meant to be. The basic perversion of this capacity is redirecting its focus onto ourselves. The perverted love of reason causes us to believe that in ourselves alone we are all the god we need. It is a distortion of reason and love to believe that humans are self-sufficient and fully capable of self-satisfaction.

This understanding is so alien to our cultural thought patterns that we can barely take it in. The prevailing viewpoint in modern culture tends to be exactly what Evagrius and Cassian would consider distorted reason, for our focus is so generally self-centered that we imagine ourselves to be fully self-sufficient. We *do* think that we are fully capable of self-satisfaction, limited only by information we have not yet acquired. Many of our thoughts and actions are centered on our desire for self-sufficiency. But consider for a moment: have we found abundance of life by following this course? Do we discover satisfaction and happiness as we pursue our individual purposes and isolating desires? Do we know anyone following this path who is really full of life and joy and peace?

79

Again, we must nuance our observations. It is unquestionably the case that our contemporary emphasis on self-esteem has resulted in many improvements in the overall quality of human life. We have found far too much of value in our vision of the dignity of every person to turn back from our commitment to the wholeness of the individual. But we might note that Benedict, Cassian, and Evagrius were also committed to the integrity of every soul in God's care. Benedict, for example, charges the abbot to deal with each monk differently, according to the temperament and unique qualities of each; further, he insists that every member of the community must be consulted regarding major decisions, because God often reveals to the younger what is best for all (RB, chapters 2 and 3). However, just as the community suffers when any individual is neglected, so the individuals suffer when community is disregarded; and all suffer when God is ignored. The benefit is reciprocal and mutual.

So the Rule and its sources emphasize the importance of self-surrender as well as self-esteem. Willfulness is a danger, and always to be contained; but the intent is not to break the person's will but rather to train it, so that the person gradually finds true self-valuing in the mutual communion with God that is the characteristic mark of wholeness. It is no more appropriate for us to endeavor to *be* God than it is for God to take us over completely; it is the loving relationship of two (and more) who are utterly other that brings lively fullness into being. So let us turn to the two most ominous patterns of thought, those that are perversions of reason.

80

The pattern of thoughts associated with vainglory is sometimes missing from a contemporary listing of vices, or is combined with the final category, that of pride. While the two are closely linked, they do differ. Vainglory is taking credit for everything good that happens as if we alone had caused it. We might contrast *acedia,* which is often associated with failure, to vainglory, which is often associated with success. Just as there are dangers in hitting bottom and thinking ourselves wholly unworthy, so there are also dangers in being so elated that we think ourselves the only ones who can help or mend or fix or bless. Vainglory prevents us from taking pleasure in the success of others because we insist the focus always be on our own achievements. We need constantly to be center stage, seeking ever greater signs of approval.

One form of vainglory might be the insistence that everything unfold as we think it should. Sometimes people in helping professions insist on fixing situations and people; they feel personally affronted by delay, cannot accept the possibility of genuine tragedy, and require the injured party to appear bright and happy and grateful. Perhaps a spiritual director may require her directees to demonstrate transformation on cue, just as a surgeon may need for all her patients to return quickly to full functioning. A father may be unable to accept his son's conscientious objection to a war because it seems to reject the father's heroic military service. Vainglory cannot accept that many things unfold at odds with our expectations.

Another form of vainglory is the singleminded pursuit of success, achievement, and ambition. In my own life I remember a time when I had achieved many outward signs of success but I felt no gratitude because I believed that I had worked hard for and deserved every single bit of reward I gained. I thought I was being reasonable, yet my perverted reason saw nothing beyond the boundaries of my own intent. So my heart was empty and my juices dried up; the outer applause did not touch my inner need for self-acceptance. I had to face my inability to create for myself those conditions necessary for my life to be genuinely full, and only when I surrendered to this truth did I begin to feel thankful for gifts received. Thankfulness changed my whole perspective. Genuine self-esteem is a partner of self-surrender, and both are alien to vainglory.

The ancients consistently viewed pride, the second pattern of thoughts resulting from perverted love, as the most serious and dangerous. It is basically the attempt to create our own world for ourselves, to embark on the path of perfection as we define it, and finally to separate ourselves definitively from God. In his *Divine Comedy* Dante wrote of pride as the great sin of blasphemy—contempt for God. Pride is the complete perversion of reason, for it takes our capacity for union with God and turns it inward on ourselves, centered in our own enclosed little world. If there is a God, and if our lives can only attain their intended wholeness in union with God, then we can readily see that pride is the direct route to despair and finally to madness. Theologian Simon Tugwell defines pride as "the final madness: supposing we can do anything without God."[9]

But, is there a God? We say yes, but are our lives really centered in that conviction? Are we convinced that our lives only find fulfillment in an ongoing relationship with God? Well, we may think so in principle, but even so we act as if we can depend on no one but ourselves. The pervasive habit of our culture is to think and act *as if* there were no God—or at least no God who is continuously active within human history. It is *very* difficult for us

82

today to understand how serious this prideful pattern of thinking is, for it is the dominant mode around us. The existence of God cannot be proved or demonstrated by scientific method, and science has taught us to be agnostic about what cannot be proved. Individual scientists do break through into an encounter with Mystery, finding the experience full of wonder, but the science of technology, no less than the science of bureaucracy, has no inherent way to deal with the non-verifiable. We have lost touch with possibilities for hearing, sensing, and seeing God: faith in a personal God seems increasingly incredible.

Do you find that it is easier to understand the patterns of thought appearing earlier on this list—such as greed or lust—than the later ones? The nearer we come to vainglory and pride, the less readily are we able to observe similar patterns in our own thinking. We may or may not desire to repent of gluttony, lust, and greed, but at least we recognize them. Vainglory and pride, on the other hand, are vague and shadowy concepts for us: they seem alien to our daily world. Perhaps the language of the tradition no longer has relevance for us, or perhaps we have become so enmeshed in the culture's dominant thought patterns that we no longer have the capacity to see the truth about ourselves clearly. Obviously this book leans toward the second explanation. As someone once suggested, "When I hear God speaking in a whisper I worry, because it is likely that I have stuffed my ears with too much cotton to hear the normal tones!" For many of us the tradition's concerns are indeed vitally relevant, and in understanding and claiming them as our own we are given tools that enable us to find and choose life.

As we saw at the beginning of this chapter, virtue only has meaning in relationship to a conception of the good life. In exploring the eight deadly thoughts we inevitably find ourselves back at this foundational question: what is the good? Yet very few of us pull back from the intensity of daily life often enough to ponder it. At the moment of our death, what do we want to say about our lives? What is the nature of the good life we hope to choose through the practice of virtue?

Evagrius and Cassian had well-developed answers to such questions. They had no doubt that human life was intended for "dwelling in God's tent," as Benedict puts it in his prologue to the Rule. Our inner desire for fullness of life is given as a pointer to our purpose, which is to live eternal life, starting right now. Their language may be different from what we might choose, but let us see clearly how radical that view was not only then, but now. We humans are made for God. Our good is to love God by consecrating our lives to God, serving God and doing God's will in all things. For God's will is inherently our delight, and when we choose God over and over, we are learning to honor those parts of ourselves that will bring us into abundant life.

The opposite of choosing God is choosing self-will, a turning away from God in order to live within ourselves, independent of God. Do we choose God first, or choose self first? We might wonder whether it has to be stated as such a stark choice, yet that does seem to be exactly the way the human heart works. In practice one or the other is preferred in every moment of choice. By practicing virtue, we seek in time to live more truly into the unity of God's will and our delight; we seek to learn more fully how to be who we are meant to be by following God's guidance and cherishing God's companionship. The good life for us is to love God wholly, and to love neighbor and self through God's eyes.

The Christian tradition's definition of the good life is clear: fullness of life for humans is impossible without intimacy and devoted communion between the soul and God. All work with thoughts, all practice of virtue, is a means of gaining full freedom for the ongoing praise and adora-

83

tion of God's very being, and the unfolding of our own greatest potential.

❧ Virtuous Practice

Now that we know what the vices are, we might expect to find a list of eight "good thoughts" that we can oppose to each of the troublesome ones. It would be comforting to look at two parallel lists, one of vices to be avoided matched by one of virtues to be practiced. But the monastic tradition intentionally does not provide a list of virtues, for the list of eight vices, or troubling thoughts, is not to be seen as a list of things to be avoided. Instead, each thought pattern is a continuum characterized by two extremes: one end represents too much of the thought, while the other end represents too little. Thus, for example, *both* ends of the vainglory continuum express perverted love. At one end we might find a kind of elation in which we fantasize excessive personal greatness; at the other end is deflation, in which we think we are worth nothing at all because we failed to receive any recognition in the last few hours. The goal would be to live somewhere near the midpoint of the vainglory continuum, seeing both our strengths and weaknesses realistically.

We can fruitfully pursue this imagery a little further. Imagine that what appears to be a continuum—a straight line with opposite qualities at each end—may actually be the segment of a helix or spiral. Now the line expressing each virtue is lifted up at both ends and brought around to form a slightly open circle at the top; the two previously extreme ends are adjacent and close to each other, while both are far away from the midpoint of the line (now the bottom of the circle). The circularity of the helix segment suggests that the extremes of the two endpoints actually have more in common with each other than either has to the middle.

84

With anger, for example, at one pole we see assault and violence and at the other a helpless surrender to any show of force. Bring both ends round to create a spiral, and then we have violence and lack of resistence side by side, with both as far as possible from firmness of purpose in the center. If I were troubled by the anger thought pattern, I would first try to become aware of my habitual tendency: Do I usually choose attack or collapse? Either way, the best practice for me is to direct my response more toward the midpoint, where virtue resides. At this point our image of the helix can go no further, because the thought patterns do not suggest an absolute midpoint to be reached and settled into for all time. Instead, our ongoing work is to live creatively with the tension between opposites for a healthy internal vigor, trusting in the Holy Spirit to help us make the appropriate modifications.

85

This work is quite difficult, and is often best assisted by a guide or spiritual director because it is easy to deceive ourselves about where we stand. For example, let's say that I am struggling with the fact that I am giving so much energy to my work in service of others, such as counseling (which I "love"—or maybe lust for) that I never take time to nurture myself (whom I would just as soon ignore anyway). If I begin to think about finding ways to give more energy to myself, my mind is likely to allege that I am horribly selfish and uncaring even to consider reducing my commitment to those in need. While selfishness may be the quality at the opposite end of the lust continuum, I am most unlikely to sin in that direction at this time, because of my deeply ingrained tendency to discount my own needs. On the other hand, if I continually ignore the need for self-care, I may find myself easily jumping the small gap between extremes into total burnout, where I no longer have the resources to care for myself or anyone else. Short and incremental moves toward the center of the continuum are the healthiest strategy, and a spiritual guide can help us trust the desire to choose them. In the example we are using that means small but deliberate steps to include self-nurture regularly within, say, a weekly schedule.

Thus we see that the list of troubling thoughts is a more comprehensive list than we have imagined, because it contains within itself directions for practice, depending on the particular focus each of us needs at the moment. Accordingly, those qualities which we commonly think of as virtues are *not* meant to be set alongside the list of troubling thoughts and substituted for them. Rather, the virtues are those qualities that help us make the ongoing discernments required to train our thoughts toward God.

CHAPTER 4

Benedict and Virtue

I call heaven and earth to witness against you today that I have set before you life and death, blessings and curses. Choose life so that you and your descendants may live, loving the LORD your God, obeying him, and holding fast to him. (Deuteronomy 30:19-20)

If virtue is character, its aim is the good life. St. Benedict readily follows Evagrius and Cassian in their description of virtue. God's will is our delight, our very life. The goal of virtue is to learn to prefer God in every moment, and this brings us fullness of life because our joy and wholeness is founded in intimacy and devoted communion with God. Having developed character through the practice of virtue, we are free to choose life.

Let us then turn more specifically to Benedict's insights about virtue and choosing the good life, which are explicitly addressed in the Rule itself. Although Benedict clearly admires the insights of Evagrius and Cassian, even telling his monks to read and study Cassian's writings, his own rule has the barest minimum discussion of virtue and vice. Since virtue is so central to the practice of the Christian life, we would expect at least a short chapter on the subject. Yet we know Benedict likes to eliminate detail in order to focus on the heart of the matter, and he does just that with virtue. Recognizing that virtue is fundamentally about our relationship with God, Benedict centers on the primary term used to describe the Christian's relationship with God: humility. He summarizes the extensive body of Cassian's thought about the practical life in his own, relatively short chapter seven on humility. As always, Benedict draws directly on Cassian's own writings and on the *Rule of the Master,* a rule written by an anonymous author in the sixth or seventh century.[1] Benedict stands firmly in the tradition, but selects and organizes to add his own emphases.

According to the Benedictine scholar Adalbert de Vogue, it is impossible to attribute too much importance to Benedict's chapter on humility.[2] In it, Benedict traces the whole spiritual life, beginning with obedience out of fear of God's wrath and developing gradually the perfect delight of charity. Benedict concludes the whole doctrinal part of the Rule in this chapter on the twelve degrees of humility, which embraces all that has preceded it. Humility summarizes the spirituality of the Rule, rooting itself in the word of Christ, "Those who humble themselves will be exalted" (Luke 14:11). For Benedict, humility is the means beyond all others by which we grow in the essential relationship with God that alone enables fullness of life. Through humility, we become the kind of person we long to be.

This is a radical idea, and we must ease into it gradually, for it goes strongly against the grain. In Greek thought, humility was considered a shame rather than a virtue; likewise, in contemporary thought, humility is often regarded as unhealthy self-abasement. If our own goal is to integrate a healthy self-esteem with a joyful self-surrender, we might think that it would be more helpful to avoid the language of humility altogether. But it holds too important a place in Benedict's synthesis for us to set it aside. Instead, in our endeavor to see as Benedict sees, we must engage humility at the heart of the virtuous life.

Humility is linked to the Latin word *humus,* meaning earth or soil, and to "human," whom we say was created our of the moist loam of earth. An essential aspect of humility is the acceptance of our creatureliness, the recognition not only that *we* are not God, but also that we *need* God for our survival and our flourishing. In scripture, God's *anawim*—the lowly ones—are considered to be especially blessed because they know they need God in everything. Humility is facing the truth about our human condition, accepting our limitations, and cheerfully depending on God. This is a very difficult task, for we are always striving for self-sufficiency, always thirsting for power and control. The reason Benedict suggests that monastics should "seek humbling experiences" (RB 58:7) is that they help constrain our persistent pride. There is no virtue in believing ourselves to be unconstrained, unlimited, able to think and do anything, because it is simply not the truth. Humility is acceptance of the groundedness, the "earthed" nature of human being, our particularity.

89

Humility is *recognizing the truth.* We are beings whose lives are framed by death, limitation, failure, failing short. Maturity involves recognizing these realities without disgust and despair. To look death and limitation in the face and *still* aspire to the greatness for which we are destined in Christ: this is humility. Knowing the truth about ourselves involves awareness of both our strengths and weaknesses, and of the fact that God sees both clearly. In truth, we notice how enslaved we are to ego, comfort, control. Oddly enough, we can pretend to ourselves that we do not share these basic human weakness *until* we begin to long for and draw near to the Holy One, and in the clear light of that Presence we sorrowfully realize how great is the distance between us and the One we love.

The good intentions smashed so decisively in my spontaneous outburst of anger, the utter incapacity to be generous to someone who consistently rubs me the wrong way—how tangled I am in my own sin! The needless deaths of precious children, the gleeful displays of revenge in public affairs, the widening circles of environmental devastation caused by an automobile-dependent society— how many ways there are to see our own limitations! The temptation is to do one of two things: either to give up in despair and ignore further evidence of this truth, or to join the fray and defeat everyone else at the game. Humility insists that we do neither, requiring instead that we first face the truth, especially about ourselves, and then constantly ask God's power to forgive and heal our brokenness.

If humility counteracts pride, it equally counteracts despair. We can refuse relationship with God by thinking too little of ourselves no less than by thinking too much. We are not to concentrate only on our sinfulness to the exclusion of the awareness of divine mercy. To believe ourselves worth nothing at all is to ignore God's loving intentions for our life. To despair or to allow ourselves to be crushed with shame is to defy God no less than to inflate ourselves. We must face our potential for greatness no less than our creatureliness, in the full practice of humility. We must learn to live fully in hope of the grace and mercy of God. The truth, which we discover daily, must include the awareness that each tiny miracle of the created world—ourselves included—is bursting with the possibility of fruitfulness in the Spirit, as well as situated within given limitations. Humility involves holding in tension *both* consciousness of our own imperfections *and* joyful living with confidence in God's mercy. The feeling

of humility is to stand securely grounded in earth, with
arms lifted upward toward heaven, sensing the dynamic
energy created when the two countervailing forces
embrace as they meet in our center. We are creatures,
called to share the divine life, as Jesus Christ taught us in
his way of being.

Our humility is founded in God's own humility. God's   91
own self is wholly self-giving, wholly in relationship with
us. As the psalmist says to God in one translation of Psalm
18:35, "Your humility has made me great." It is God's
hand and heart outstretched to us that calls us into being
in the first place, and that continually draws us to surpass
ourselves in the loving relationship with God. God is
wholly self-giving, as we see not only in Jesus (see John
13:3-5 and Philippians 2:5-11) but also within the very
mystery of the Trinity itself, which is a unity of three self-
giving persons whose love overflows into creation. God so
loves us that in some way we are made lovable; God enters
our own limited experience and that presence transforms
us, enabling us to be what we have longed to be. Humility
is a way—perhaps the best way—of learning more about
the fully human life God has in mind for us.

Let us then turn specifically to chapter seven of
Benedict's Rule, called the "ladder of humility" because it
refers to Jacob's dream of the ladder to heaven (Genesis
28:12). Each of the steps in that ladder is first paraphrased
in what follows and then reflected upon in an effort to
interpret the spiritual import of Benedict's core virtue in
contemporary language.

❧ The Inward Steps of Humility

Step 1: Keep the fear of God before my eyes, fleeing
every kind of forgetfulness. (RB 7:10)

Benedict's lengthy discourse on the first step of humility
shows us where the roots of humility are planted—in the

fear of God. Fundamentally, humility is the recognition that to be human is to be *created,* that is, to be in relationship with a Creator. It is to know oneself fundamentally dependent on and interdependent with a Reality, so far beyond our capacity to imagine as to cause us to tremble. In Benedict's time, the whole Christian world had recently gone through strenuous upheaval in the passionate debates surrounding the Arian heresy, which asked whether Jesus really was God. Thus we notice that Benedict never refers to "Jesus" with simple familiarity; for Benedict, God is the high and lofty One who inhabits eternity, and Jesus is Lord.

Notice the frequency with which, when the angel of the Lord appears in scripture, the first words are, "Do not be afraid." Even in the first Pentecost community "awe came upon everyone" (Acts 2:43) as they were seized by the glory and nearness of God. We might well ponder, what is there to fear? What is this fear, so near to love, so close to the Holy? A wonderful irony resides in the human heart: *we often most fear what we most desire or long for.* For example, I long to find a true friend of the heart, but in an actual friendship, as we begin to move toward those deeper levels of intimacy where I lose control of what is happening between us, I often find occasion to pick a fight. Or, I really want to lose weight, but as I get near my goal, I go on an eating binge. That which we deeply desire is ordinarily something which, by definition, we cannot produce for ourselves; if we could make it happen, we would not have to long for it. Thus, in order for our desires to be fulfilled, we inevitably become vulnerable to unknown and unanticipated possibilities. In a real sense, it is just those unimaginable possibilities for which we dream, but when they actually draw near, we feel fear.

This paradoxical pattern of desire and fear is especially noticeable in our relationship with God. Can you imagine being afraid of God? Some people cannot—God is too much the loving companion and father, while others feel only fear—their human authority figures have been punishing, and so God is seen that way, too. Neither image really comes close to what is meant by fear of God. The biblical term necessarily includes an awareness that God is all-loving Creator, but it also suggests that God is "great and awesome" (Deuteronomy 7:21). Perhaps this fear is something like the awe (and terror) of watching an ocean storm or a wild brushfire; perhaps it is like feeling the hair rise on our necks when we encounter the uncanny.

93

Possibly we do not know how to fear God nowadays because we have lost a sense of wonder. What an astonishing thing it is to be a living being! What a miracle is birth, as new parents must marvel in the hours after their child is born. Children know how "magically" a cut heals; what a wonder is the unity and wisdom of the body itself! Who indeed is the One who can create such miracles out of nothingness? What have I to do with such a One? Fear is indeed an appropriate response to such majesty, such power, such love.

Sometimes images and metaphors can help us understand more deeply than words a wondrous and mysterious reality. Once in prayer when I was feeling fearful, I was given an image that continues to sustain me. I felt myself to be a newborn colt, standing alone in a paddock where the morning mist surrounded and softened all shapes. Cold and alone, I shivered. At the edge of the fog, I could make out a human shape approaching me, hand outstretched to touch and gently caress. While I knew that the person meant me no harm, I could not contain the fear rising in me at this approach, and my shivering increased uncontrollably. I *wanted* to wait to be touched, and I also wanted to bolt. In that moment, the only thing I could do was *not to run*. And that was all that God asked of me; that was enough.

We may normally respond to an underlying fear, companion of our desire, as an impediment preventing us from choosing life. But when we understand the pivotal role fear plays in the unfolding of desire, we learn that it can actually help us remain present to the awesome power of the Divine Life drawing near to help us. And we notice, too, that even more than we fear the presence of the Mighty One, we fear the absence. For at the deepest levels of our being, we long for and rejoice in the presence of God, who not only gives life, but in love makes life worth living.

94

Step 2. Love not my own will; rather do God's will. (RB 7:31-32)

The second, third, and fourth steps of Benedict's ladder to heaven involve the training of our own will. As we noted earlier, Benedict focuses spiritual discipline and the practice of virtue on disposing our wills toward God's will for us. The objective of this training is not to root out and destroy personal will, but rather to teach ourselves to recognize and follow the path that will enable us to live fully as we desire. We substitute the willingness to find and follow that delight for a willful insistence on our own way. In a certain sense, the untrained soul is like a young child not wanting to go to sleep, insisting on her right to stay up, unaware that she will enjoy tomorrow much more if she sleeps well tonight. God gives us the means to discipline, to teach, to show our wills the good for us, and we can learn to trust that God's will indeed is our delight.

Our work is to direct our focus, to center our vision on God. In prayer we gaze in adoration on God, and in daily life we seek God within and beyond everything in the created order. We are endeavoring to focus on God and keep our attention there. This is difficult because ordinarily we are so wrapped up in ourselves that we forget that God's will might be an alternative center, established within our being. All the normal clues of our culture direct us outward—to our many possessions, to longed-for successful results, to a scattered and undisciplined reaction to external stimuli. In our time as in Benedict's, it is an extraordinarily difficult thing to shift our inner center of focus to God. And, of course, the point is that we *cannot* do it with our own willing; we must give up our will, surrendering to God's, and receive the gift of humility that comes with such surrender.

Self-will is a deliberate turning away from God, chosen again and again in our daily routines. The central issue of humility is choosing God first or choosing self first. One choice or the other is in practice *preferred* in every moment of decision.

Benedict is succinct here. No doubt that is partly because so much of his guidance throughout the Rule is oriented toward this problem, which is at the heart of the spiritual life as he sees it. He says two simple things. He turns our attention toward Christ, then he tells us to watch him, be nourished by him, and let him lead us. As an example he makes a peculiar reference to Irene, a Christian martyr who died in 304 C.E. Benedict is apparently using a quotation from the *Acta Anastasiae,* in which Irene, when threatened with forcible prostitution, replies that, as with those forced to eat meat sacrificed to idols, this would be no act of sin if done under "necessity," but would win her a crown.[3] There is some confusion about the exact wording of the quotation and therefore about its meaning. But we can take it that when Irene was faced with the hard demands of martyrdom, she sought God in their midst, asking what in this situation was essential for her to learn. It was her conviction that a loving God met her in every time and place, and her only responsibility was to look for and welcome God everywhere. In doing so she could be at rest, even in those most extreme conditions.

96

Step 3. Submit to my superior for the love of God.
(RB 7:34)

Difficult as it is, I prefer to surrender my will to God rather than to another person. But Benedict wants us to understand the importance of completely releasing any residual responsibility we think we may have for the universe. The point is not to give up our conscience, not to offer mindless compliance, but rather to release the secret belief that we know better than anyone else. To help us in this difficult task, Benedict suggests that we keep our eyes on Christ. Did Christ have any human superiors? What might it mean to say we are imitating Christ in submitting to human superiors? Benedict quotes Philippians 2 as saying that Jesus was obedient unto death, so apparently the human "superiors" to which he refers are the secular and religious authorities who unjustly condemned Jesus to death. Can Benedict really mean that we have a spiritual duty to submit to such treatment?

Obviously, every spiritual action takes discernment, humility no less than any other. Obviously, too, there are times when we are called to challenge civil authority with our very lives, and our century alone has seen the courageous acts of many Christians in that regard. So submission may also involve challenge. Certainly any submission in humility must be both freely chosen and undertaken for the love of God. These two essential conditions create the reconciling power of submission. Suppose a monastic superior gives an order that appears to be both arbitrary and against the best interests of a monastic: perhaps the monk must abandon college studies to return to the monastery for a job that someone else could do equally well. The superior's action itself is not automatically beneficial or grace-filled for the monk and the community. However, when the subordinate freely consents to accept the decision for the love of God, then even the harshest decision can become an instrument for God's healing love, for everyone involved. This is not a "fact" that makes sense to the rational mind, but at times the heart can understand it well.

97

The scripture passage Benedict has chosen to guide us here is the beautiful hymn from Philippians: "Let the same mind be in you that was in Christ Jesus" (2:5-11). We find in this poem one of the images of ascending and descending central to Benedict's chapter on the "ladder" of humility, emphasizing that the actions of humility are to be taken out of love. It is love, not hatred or resentment, that is to motivate our relations with other persons. We are to try to live first of all in the awareness that God loves even our enemies with the same cherishing tenderness that God has for us. In the awareness of this love, our own desires are set in context.

Our goal in the practice of virtue is to choose life, to orient ourselves to the fullness of life we desire. Yet as we know, some desires distract us from the great desire for life. This third step of humility shows one way we can train our desires toward the one thing necessary. Superficially, we might incline toward pleasure and influence. But by consenting to be obedient and listen attentively, we learn to discipline our own desires in relation to the wishes of another. We freely consent to be attuned to the natural limitations and checks on individual desire that are always provided by life with others. We consent to these human limitations *for the love of God*. Which is to say, we look to every barrier, every constraint, every order, everything that stands in our way or does not make sense—we look to all of these as ways in which God can be greeted and honored in our daily life. For the love of God, we consecrate desire. We let our many little desires be gradually enfolded into the one great desire for God.

98

Step 4. In difficult circumstances, embrace suffering and endure without weakening or giving up. (RB 7:35-36)

The fourth step of humility gathers together and brings to culmination the ideas initiated in steps two and three on the training of the will. Benedict calls us to embrace hard things and to endure. Just as the foundations of humility are found in the fear of God, so the essential disposition of the will is toward *patience*. Both concepts are alien to our culture.

The Latin verb from which patience is derived, *patior*, refers to suffering. Suffering usually means to be acted upon in a manner that is painful, as in "she suffered from a continuous cough." The same Latin root also gives us our word "passion," which essentially means to be acted upon (or taken over by) by a strong emotion, such as anger or lust. Both meanings are integrated when we speak of the "passion of Christ," which refers to his painful suffering at the hands of the Romans, along with his intense conviction that God required this of him as an expression of love.[4]

Two additional qualities of patience are revealed by Jesus in his final days. The first is that he endures the necessary suffering without complaint or murmuring. Jesus' patience, his passion, is not indifferent to the situation, but is nonetheless without rage or discontent. This is a delicate balance—to be filled with purpose, yet to be willing to hand it over, serene in the certainty of God's governance of the world. The second quality, which flows from the first, is the inner freedom to let events unfold as they will, not limiting our patience to those outcomes we can control, but enduring even when outcomes are unpredictable because of our abiding confidence in the providence of God.

What do we think fullness of Christian life is like? Do we imagine that once we have committed our lives to God in Christ, God will protect us and bring us blessings? While this is true, it is important not to interpret protection and blessing in too narrow a way. Like all human life, our Christian life will no doubt be full of setbacks, "contraries," hardships, injuries, and all manner of difficult, unfavorable, and unjust conditions. Benedict directs our attention not only to the suffering our Lord had to endure, but also to St. Paul's sufferings on behalf of Christ. We are not to seek suffering, but simply to be aware that it is likely that life itself will test our commitment to this simple way, even and especially those closest to us (Matthew 10:21-22). In fact, we may sometimes find ourselves asking how our motives and actions can have any effect at all if we cannot achieve results that bring public acceptance. What good will our death—literal or metaphorical—do? How can we help God if we are fired from our job, or become so isolated or marginal that all we can do is pray?

When we are not achieving "results" in our pursuit of virtue and character, are we still following God? How are we to respond to suffering and even defeat? That is the question this step of humility answers. Embrace suffering and endure. Be patient. Let your consciousness be silent. Wait for the Lord. This step of humility is related to our our aggressive energies, our refusing powers. Our discipline is to focus these energies not on lashing out in anger, but rather on the more flexible and long-lasting affirmation that is implied by endurance.

What enables and empowers endurance is the awareness that God is met in suffering no less than in joy. When we embrace hardship, we are embracing Christ found within the hardship. The patience of humility is made possible in the confidence and joy expressed by St. Paul in his letter to the Romans: love is stronger than death. What profound freedom is expressed by one able to live in this way!

100

Step 5. Confess sinful thoughts and secret wrongs, and receive forgiveness. (RB 7: 44-48)

The next three steps of humility are associated with knowing ourselves. In the fifth step we give up the need to be above reproach. One of the most useful tools of pride is to make sure that others think well of us. It can be relatively easy to *seem* holy to others, and to persuade ourselves that we really are so. We can identify so strongly with the expectations that we suppress the truth about our inner struggles, even from ourselves. This element of humility involves honest self-appraisal and a willingness to speak to another about the dismaying chaos of our inner world.

Speaking aloud of our fears and sinful impulses puts them in perspective, and prevents them from gaining too strong a hold on us. Benedict loves to use the horrifying image of Psalm 137, that of dashing babies against rocks, to signify what we ought to do with temptations: while our impulses are still small, they are to be thrown at the feet of Christ, our rock. Often, when we do not speak of these impulses, they begin to grow and take on a life of their own inside us, drawing us nearer to acting out the sin itself. As we saw in our exploration of troubling thoughts, the Christian tradition urges us not to conceal any of the important inner motions; it is better to let the light of God illumine them by confessing them to another human being. When thoughts are out in the open in this way they lose their power over us, and we are better able to receive the cleansing and healing power of God's ever-present love. Notice that it is not just confession but *forgiveness* that is an important element here. Do not be too proud to receive God's mercy, whatever your sinful secrets. Confession implies acceptance both of our own sinfulness *and* of God's mercy.

101

Step 6. Be content with the most common and worst of everything. (RB 7:49)

The essence of this step of humility is to accept interiorly all the conditions of one's being and one's life, whatever they are—to learn to "be content." Discontent often is caused by ambition, the constant endeavor to become more influential or more lovable than we inherently are. How difficult it is for us not to try to justify ourselves by parading before others, those credentials or accomplishments we mistakenly believe give us value. Yet, when we genuinely accept that without God we are nothing, how much contentment we can enjoy. For in God's eyes we are fully known and of infinite value, not because we are "important" but because we are loved. Until we accept this truth, we are always trying to put on a better show, to cover over the inadequate self.

This step naturally follows that of confession, because we need first to accept ourselves as we are before we can be content. So often when we seek external validation we are trying to cover over some incompleteness in ourselves. So often when we meddle with or try to "fix" something or somebody, we are seeking to avoid facing the limitations of our lives. Can we genuinely accept that we have nothing—not a single quality, not a single possession— that does not come to us as a gift of God? If we can genuinely accept this, then pride is on its way out, and humility is indeed opening us to the glorious reality that, no matter how little we are, God is with us always.

102

The key to contentment is gratitude. When we can begin the day by expressing thanks to God for whatever gifts are given us in this moment, then our capacity for contentment increases. This is not to be artificial and contrived; we should not give thanks for things that appall and anger us. Rather, it is building the capacity to notice and value those things for which we are grateful, even in the worst of situations. It is to recognize the many things we can appreciate that we have received unmerited. The more thanks we give, the more we see things for which we are thankful. Gratitude builds our capacity to receive the gifts of God, and deepens our receptivity to contentment.

Step 7. Even in my heart, be willing to depend utterly on God's mercy. (RB 7:51-54)

Steps five through seven involve honest self-appraisal. In step five I accept that I do not control what comes into my mind and heart, only what I do with it when it arrives. In step six I accept that my only value is in relation to God's unlimited love for me. Difficult as these two steps are, I am tempted to undertake them only with my mind, holding aside a few reservations, keeping to myself a secret place in my heart that says, "I am different and special." My response of rebellion to this third repetition of utter dependence on God reminds me that I have not yet completely surrendered to the truth. I still want to be perfect and wonderful, surprising God with how great I am on my own! The repetition, the constant return to the simple center of value, is necessary in order to reach our *hearts*. It is not enough to understand with our minds, or even to act with our tongues and our hands; the truth of humility must be enshrined in the heart. We need to return to the truth over and over again, never forgetting that God is God and our worth rests in being beloved of God.

We have said that humility is recognizing the truth. It is hard work to stand firm, gazing honestly at the truth of personal limits and weakness while remembering that God knows all and loves us still. And yet this is only half of humility. The other half is to persevere in seeking to surpass ourselves, with God's help. We are to be realistic about our potential even while gazing fearlessly at our limitations. This seems confusing and emotionally unsettling, almost off-balance, because in this middle place we are subject both to self-disgust and to vainglory. Holding simultaneous awareness of our own flaws along with our aspirations is so troublesome that we often choose to distract ourselves by "forgetting" one, settling in the less challenging corner of either self-disgust or false elation. Even more tempting is the distraction provided by judging the failures of other people. How satisfying it is to create a "safe place" for ourselves by comparing our spiritual progress with others who are doing even worse!

Humility teaches that suffering can purify us by paring away every safety or pleasure with which we insulate ourselves. Suffering can be brought on by external pressures but can equally be caused by the internal anguish of standing naked before the all-seeing eye of God. Having lost the masks we usually wear to protect ourselves, we are distraught, often endeavoring like Adam and Eve to hide in the bushes of deceit. But God rejoices in our humility, already running to clothe us in the raiment of Love, which we are unable to wear until vulnerability fits us for the gift uniquely our own. The task of humility is to think rightly of ourselves, according to our gifts. Strength and weakness are both gifts.

The wonderful and heartening wisdom of true humility is that ultimately it suggests the integration of the best of what we know about the importance of self-esteem with the best of what we know about the importance of self-surrender. Psychological health demands that we know ourselves to be precious, valuable, loved, just as we are. Spiritual health demands that we surrender ourselves in willing commitment to something greater than ourselves, to God and God's purposes, to Mystery beyond our understanding, in such a way that we are able to transcend our limitations and particularities. Too often we think of self-esteem and self-surrender as opposites, incompatible principles. Yet in our hearts we sense that we need both, and that to forego either one is a severe loss. Humility teaches us a way to integrate the best of both foundational principles necessary to the living of a full human life.

⨭ The Outward Steps of Humility

Steps one through seven of humility help us cultivate the interior disposition of purity of heart, and thus pertain primarily to our inner experience of who we are and what is our relationship with God. The remaining five steps in Benedict's list pertain more to exterior dimensions, or outward practices, of humility. Perhaps we might wonder why we should care what others see or think of us, since humility is fundamentally a matter between the person and God. In the Rule, the outward observances are not designed primarily so that others will think well of us, but are rather given as practices, habits that help form our inner dispositions.

Let's take a moment to see how this can work. We can learn the virtue of humility in two quite different ways—inner and outer—and Benedict suggests we work on both. In the inner practice described in steps one through seven,

104

we start from a decision that humility is of value for us, and we choose to practice it in accordance with that decision. But we can also do it the other way around. In the outward practice, we faithfully *act as if* we were humble, hoping our actions themselves will teach us inwardly what is valuable for us.

In certain matters, especially when experience itself is important, it is difficult if not impossible to understand what is sought until it has been practiced for a time. This is particularly true of prayer and spiritual formation. If someone asks what actually happens when we experience God, there is no way to give a full answer. We can approximate, suggest metaphors, point in a general direction. But the answer can only be understood when the heart of the questioner has expanded sufficiently to receive the personal touch of God. There is no shortcut to the result, no way to mimic or copy the experience for one unwilling to walk the path personally.

Anyone can imitate virtuous behavior, outwardly appearing to be moderate in food and drink, chaste, and generous. However, if while displaying such behavior our thoughts are filled with greed and self-righteousness, we have gained nothing, and indeed have lost ground toward the goal of becoming whole, holy beings. The point of the practice of the virtues is to become a certain kind of person rather than to succeed in any external goals. But paradoxically the kind of person we seek to become is not fully known to us until we have become that person. We must trust the judgment of someone whose life we respect that virtue is valuable, and then surrender our will fully to the practice. If we do this, even without understanding completely what we are doing or why, we gladly discover that over time the virtue does indeed become a welcome inner disposition.

Commitment to a steady outward practice of virtue can train our will beyond the understanding of our minds.

105

106

A practice, or outward form, is a way of accepting and living with the limits of creaturely life.[5] Because the practice is not of our own making but taught by and received from others, certain elements will inevitably feel artificial and arbitrary. Practice is artificial because it sets constraints and boundaries on freedom; it is arbitrary because it is always possible to find another method that is arguably superior. But we must make a commitment to a specific form or practice if we hope to realize the goal we seek. Another way to say this is that we must make choices to attain the fullness of life we desire. Because we are creatures, we must accept necessary limits as the form from within which our wholeness can emerge. One of the great traps of pride is the illusion that we do not need to limit ourselves or to make choices for—like God—we can have it all. So we refuse to choose, not realizing even that is a choice. Usually, refusal to choose means avoiding the possibility of creaturely wholeness.

Desires become fruitful only when tested against the problems that inevitably arise in disciplined practice. The means by which the practice teaches us character is by resisting our will and baffling our understanding. To be faithful to practice means to continue steadfastly even when we can neither explain nor remedy the trouble. In that steadfastness, we wait and listen and find ourselves opened to deeper realities than we knew.

Commitment to practice can help ease the initial struggle involved in training the heart by removing the focus from thoughts and feelings and emphasizing simple outward (and thus inward) persistence. Those who have decided to quit smoking will recognize the pattern of initially wanting a cigarette every second, then finding the intervals increasing to every five seconds and every twenty seconds. That first minute is a very long one, but within a few days, ten minutes can pass before they think of a cigarette. In two weeks, an intense and urgent desire to smoke may surface occasionally, but it too will pass. In time they know themselves to be non-smokers. Perhaps the "thought" of a cigarette will return from time to time over many years, but habits of mind have been created to deal with the thought. It is no shame to receive the initial impulse, but we seek not to let it linger, but rather, as Benedict says, to cast it in its infancy at the rock of Christ (RB Prologue 28, 4:50). The practice of virtue involves a willingness always to be a beginner; always to surrender to practice again. The practice itself can teach and sustain us.

107

Step 8. Follow the common rule and example. (RB 7:55)

Benedict begins this section on outward practice with the reminder that we share a common life, that we live side by side with others who are struggling interiorly with much the same issues as those we face. Let me not hide from others, or embark on a life with God in isolation from others, but rather recognize that what the others know and do is of inestimable help to me. Let me not strive for singularity, to be seen to be better (or worse) than others, but to be willing to belong, to be a part of this particular human community to which I have been given. Community is healthful for us both as a challenge to our pride, and also as a wise source of strength. Community is a repository of tradition and practice that can sustain us greatly in times of difficulty.

It may startle us to be reminded that humility is a communal enterprise, for we have been focused on the interior disposition of humility, which is largely a personal matter. But always, as both Benedict and the gospel remind us, living as a Christian is fundamentally a matter of living a common life with others equally beloved by God. Authentic humility rests in respect for one another.

108   Step 9. Practice silence. (RB 7:56-58)

The final three steps of humility all have to do with limiting speech—or perhaps more aptly, with the quality of attentive listening for God. We have seen that humility is primarily a matter of right relationship with God and others. Too often our interactions with others are defined primarily through speech, even in our prayer where we tell or ask God what is going on. The mark of a humble life is focused, respectful listening to everything—one's body and inner motives, the environment, the sorrows and joys of others—and hearing in all God's compassionate voice.

I love the thought attributed to John of the Cross, "God spoke one word, and that Word was his Son. The word was spoken in eternal silence, and in silence must it be heard." Attentive silence, or not speaking much, is the best way to be attuned to the empowering presence of God in our midst. Even when we receive a glorious insight, it is often good to wait before speaking, allowing ideas to take root in our depths rather than be dissipated too soon. Let our consciousness prefer silence, that we may receive the Holy Spirit's strength in its wholeness deep in our inner beings.

Step 10. Do not be easily moved to excitement. (RB 7:59)

The specific requirement here is that one is "not easily moved to laughter," but laughter here means susceptibility to emotional highs and lows. The image that comes to mind is that found in Ephesians, where Paul encourages members of the church in Ephesus not to be "children, tossed to and fro and blown about by every wind of doctrine" (4:14). Benedict is talking here about the difference between a wise person and a fool. We are urged to cultivate the disposition of silence in order to let wisdom be formed deep within us. A fool does not let himself reach those depths, rather staying on the surface, being tossed back and forth by every wave of emotion that passes by. There is a suggestion of coarseness, a kind of base jesting that borders on the abusive: such hilarity is often used to create an artificial comradeship that is ultimately divisive because it denies the reality of God's sensitive loving in the midst of ordinary daily routines. Eliminating such "harmless" repartee from community experience may seem unnecessarily prudish until we remember Benedict's basic principle of "never forgetting." God is here. God is now. Not that God is ever solemn and heavy—after all, joy is the truest sign of the presence of God—rather, God is mysterious and wonderful and ennobling to everything touched by that Presence.

109

Step 11. Speak wisely. (RB 7:60-61)

The eleventh step gives the positive side of the two previous steps: if we are asked to be silent and not easily moved, is there some positive way we should use speech? Yes, Benedict answers: speak wisely. He gives us several marks of wise speaking: gentleness, simplicity, brevity, reasonableness. In a sense, wisdom as well as humility is summed up in these few characteristics.

Gentleness is a quality central to the enduring strength of our Lord Christ: "I am gentle and humble in heart, and

you will find rest for your souls" (Matthew 11:29).
Simplicity urges us not to waste energy on frivolous
things, nor to take ourselves too seriously, but to focus on
delight in God. Brevity tells us that when our words are
formed in silence, they can be communicated without
complexity. And reasonableness is the capacity to let all
the qualities of our minds, including imagination and
memory, be centered in service of God. In short, let our
speech be shaped by the Holy Spirit's guidance within.

110

∰

Step 12. Let the humility of my heart be manifest in
my bearing. (RB 7:62)

The detailed language Benedict uses in this step may be
difficult for us, since we will usually not express humility
in our bodies in the same way as in those living in the sixth
century. We may be more concerned to prevent osteo-
porosis with good posture than to demonstrate humility
with a constantly bowed head. We may praise God's wonder more fully with eyes wide open to the marvels of
nature than with downcast eyes. The shift in physical
expression, however, does not negate the underlying point
with which we can sympathize: mind, body, heart, and
spirit all must be in harmony, equally expressing the com-
pleteness of our commitment to remembering God's presence in every moment. We are seeking to allow the virtue
of humility to be so foundational to our way of life that it
is *always* evident (v. 62). Humility is fundamentally not a
set of actions, but growth into a relationship of love that
expresses itself in every aspect of life.

Above all, humility is growth into that perfect love
which casts out fear. Humility is like being in love: we can
never forget it, even for a moment, because our bodies are
always reminding us: we have a lightness of heart, a spring

in our step, an eagerness for the future. We can start with inward motives and move toward outward actions, and we can also let our outward actions modify our inward spirit. Humility grows from both directions. These twelve steps of humility are not so much a progression as a group of indicators that assure us we are on the right track in our journey of ascending-by-descending toward God.

111

In this final step of humility, Benedict uses the image of the publican from Luke 18, which is also a helpful way to end our discussion of Benedict's central virtue. The parable is a familiar one: two people go up to the temple to pray. The Pharisee is full of self-righteousness, while the publican (tax collector) merely asks for mercy. Jesus tells us the publican has the purer prayer, and by this he gives us a vivid image of humility. In his prayer, the publican expresses tears and heartfelt devotion. The publican is bringing his whole self, at the deepest level of his awareness, to God, and he weeps for his sins. The publican *knows he needs God.*

This simple parable can bring great comfort to us. It suggests that there *is* a possibility and a promise of receiving what we so much long for and are so completely unable to produce for ourselves. We cannot create for ourselves that unity of Spirit wherein we find fullness of life. We cannot force our character to become virtuous. Sometimes, the harder we work at it, the more lost, alone, and fearful we feel. But there is hope in humility. Hope comes with willingness to endure in the awareness of our own neediness and dependence upon the mercy of God. When I come to prayer as one who weeps, I am where I need to be.

PART THREE

Ethics

CHAPTER 5

Living with
Wisdom and Virtue

*What is it that Yahweh asks of you, only this: That
you act justly, that you love tenderly, and that you
walk humbly with your God. (Micah 6:8[1])*

In light of what we have seen of wisdom and virtue in
the Christian tradition, it could be said that an ethical
life is an abundant life, lived according to the insights of
wisdom and the practices of virtue. In this chapter we will
explore what such a definition of ethics might mean for
us, practically speaking.

This book began by focusing on the deep-seated desire
many of us feel for fullness of life, asking whether this
continual longing for something more was problem or
promise. The pervasive sense of feeling adrift, of not really
knowing how to integrate the traditional language of
faith with the restlessness we often experience—this is definitely problem. However, the recognition that something
is missing can also be promise, if we see it as pointing us

116

toward the reintegration of lost treasures into our lives. We are often unable to learn how to live abundantly because of powerful cultural paradigms that prevent us from seeing alternative perspectives. In this book we have tried to remove some of those masks by offering modern translations of ancient Judeo-Christian insights—shifts in perspective that can illuminate possibilities for abundance.

In part one we saw that wisdom is at heart the desire for life, seeking in experience itself a coherent language of meaning revealed as the divine presence within creation. Benedict's prologue to his Rule insists that we wake up and trust the desire for life in abundance, because our Creator desires it for us also. In ongoing relationship with God, we are empowered to flourish in creative response to the desires of our hearts. Part two revealed that virtue is the training of desire by the formation of our own character, thereby strengthening our capacity to choose abundant life in accordance with our vision of the good. In the practice of virtue, we learn to turn away from means and toward deliberate choices for the good envisioned by the Creator. We become persons capable of integrating self-esteem and self-surrender. In his challenging and insightful chapter on humility, Benedict describes it as seeing ourselves rightly, both as limited creature and as beloved of God. Now, in part three, we will look specifically at the ethical situations of our daily life.

✂ Ethics as Essential to Spirituality

Ethics is about acting in accordance with what we believe. The ethical life is a life based upon moral values. Any authentic understanding of the spiritual life must inevitably deal with questions of morality and ethics, for otherwise the spirit is not embodied. Spirituality without morality is simple fantasy; spirituality *with* morality is incarnation. Biblical faith has always insisted that love of God is inseparably linked with love of neighbor as self. As the prophet Micah insists, walking with God necessarily also means acting justly to others.

In the terms we have been using, authentic relationship with the Divine Mystery involves not only wisdom (desire for the good life) and virtue (formation of personal character by choices for that good), but also ethical behavior toward the neighbor and the stranger. Unfortunately, one of the most muddled and troubling aspects of our common life today is the difficulty we have in approaching any serious and meaningful discussion of ethics. In ethics as in wisdom and virtue, we distrust the idea that anyone or anything might have any moral authority over our daily lives. And morality claims just that: *authority* about acceptable behavior. The kind of spirituality most popular today is a spirituality without morality, which offers the possibility of everyone "doing their own thing."

117

We have been asking two questions: What is fullness of life, and what is possible for human beings? Such questions need to be raised anew in our time because, in general, we have lost confidence in the traditional answers to them. Another way to say this is that we are no longer sure whether human life is capable of meaning and purpose. Many people find that the form and content expressed in traditional statements about the meaning of life have little relevance today. Either such statements are no longer credible in relation to a new world view, or they seem to be nonsense, using words that we do not even understand today. Although this loss of reliable guideposts about life is common to all times of major transition, it is still painful. When we feel adrift from meaning and purpose, we lose hope and begin to despair.

Our pattern in these chapters has been to present the desirability of an ancient value (wisdom, virtue), and then to look at the state of our culture to discern why we find it so difficult to have serious discussions about these ancient values, much less to begin incorporating them into our daily lives. In the case of ethics, which directly affects ordinary behavior, the gap between value and practice is particularly acute. Early on we identified the problematic bias in our culture against ethics as "delight in mocking the tender and the cherished." For us to look directly at the ways in which our society tends to demean ethics may be quite painful. Yet we must first see the almost invisible barriers surrounding us that make it so difficult for us to claim ethical standards for ourselves. One of these barriers is that we are so self-reliant we often believe failures to be solely our own, when we cannot meet the standards we ask of ourselves. The truth is that the predominant assumptions of our contemporary western world view make failure the most likely outcome. When we can see those assumptions clearly and challenge them, both interiorly as individuals and more deliberately as groups, we find it much easier to break through into the life of grace we desire.

✑ The Crucial Problem: Mockery of the Precious

We have seen the erosion of coherent patterns of meaning, and the increasing reliance on measures of utility rather than of value. After a time of living without connection to a usable pattern of meaning and purpose, we may forget the shock of its loss. A kind of low-level despair sets in, when we cannot find connections between our daily lives and a greater purpose, and as we cease to expect a sense of purpose to arise for us, our behavior may express an increasingly frantic urgency simply to feel *alive*. If we feel increasingly numb because of doubt about our value, we may begin to seek heightened sensory stimuli, which by their very intensity enable us to experience *something*, even if only pain or discomfort.

I live in Pasadena, and for many years we have spent at least some time on New Year's Eve on Colorado Boulevard, sharing the excitement and pleasure of the peo-

118

ple camping out overnight to await the morning's Rose
Parade. Over the years I have been here, the tone of the
street crowd has changed. A few years ago as we walked
along the street, a stranger grabbed my husband's head,
tilted it back, and poured some kind of liquid down his
throat. Doug is an easy-going man and he laughed it off as
highjinks. But it bothered me that we had no idea what
was in the concoction he had swallowed, although it
turned out my fears were groundless. Last year as we
drove along Colorado Boulevard we were aware of a high
energy level, joyful but approaching mania. As we turned
a corner, something hit my window, and almost broke it.
After a moment, I realized it was merely a spit-ball,
although thrown at close range and with considerable
force. As I reflected on what the motive for such an action
might be, I realized that there was little of value in the lives
of some of these young people. Despair turned to violence,
an inverted form of life-affirmation expressed in anything
that would give an adrenalin surge. In such a life, goodness and beauty and honor are unbearable, because the
person is effectively walled off from the experience of tenderness and vulnerability.

119

It is not easy to sit with the reality of such brutal des-
peration, yet it is increasingly noticeable. The popularity
of "shock-jocks," radio and television hosts whose repu-
tation is based on trashing respectability, tells us how
prevalent the dis-ease has become among us. The availability of books with titles like *Winning by Intimidation*
shows us how fashionable verbal cruelty has become.
Movies romanticize violence and nihilism, making killing
seem funny and cool. The cumulative effect profoundly
degrades the whole social fabric in which all of us live.

Nowadays the primary grist of political campaigns is
personal slander. What can a candidate "dig up" about an
opponent? For example, over a decade ago, we watched
without dismay while national reports openly derided

then-President Jimmy Carter for admitting that he had "lusted in his heart." President Carter's integrity in acknowledging the importance of dashing the first impulse of sin at the rock of Christ was treated not just as an old-fashioned oddity, but as a sign of his inability to exercise the necessary "strength of leadership" required of a president of the United States. Perhaps more alarming is the growing frequency of the term "damage control" to explain acceptable strategies to "spin" public perceptions so that all *seems* well.

120

The cumulative effect of all this debunking is to poison our ethical environment. We are rupturing irrevocably the connective fabric of our relationships with one another as a people. Moral values are collectively undermined by a stance that deliberately dismisses and confuses any thought or action about goodness. It is increasingly acceptable to mock any qualities that might once have been imagined to be life-giving. Ongoing verbal abuse severely damages our capacity to think clearly and act compassionately. It also greatly increases the risk in daring to speak and act ethically in such times.

While this statement of the problem may seem an over-reaction to occasional and minor events, I believe it is a pointer to where America is heading. Once these situations were more characteristic of large metropolitan areas such as Los Angeles and New York City, but they are rapidly spreading across the country, transmitted by television and the "virtual realities" of the Internet. (How much does virtual reality have in common with real virtue?) Recognizing the influences that make it difficult to treat our inner hopes and dreams and visions seriously is the first step, as Benedict learned when he left the corruption of Rome for the simplicity of his cave in the countryside around Subiaco. Benedict did not remain in Subiaco; it was a time of drawing apart to reflect honestly on the world and himself , before he founded his own community of monks seeking God. But in writing his Rule, Benedict knew that even the faith-filled members of his community brought the confusions and assumptions of the world with them, and the Rule must address such problems as an ongoing part of its communal life. Whatever moral values come to sustain us in our present day, they must be rooted in a realistic assessment of our situation.

121

The intensity of our ethical dilemma emerges from the mistaken belief that the values of the past are utterly alien to contemporary culture. But here we will endeavor to show how a genuine appropriation of the essence of Christian wisdom can actually form the nucleus of a new and more adequate way of thinking and acting ethically. The resolution is not to be found merely by holding fast to past moral values; it involves finding a way to blend the best of the old and the new. Remember the image of the shattered child's playhouse from our first chapter. Our previous way of thinking is too small for our present range of experiences; it is "dying" in order for "new life" to arise in its place. The birth of a more adequate world view is not automatic, but it is the most *likely* thing to happen, *if* wise and virtuous midwives are in place to help it gestate and emerge. For the Divine Mystery often uses death as the doorway to life, and we can be its partners if we are prepared to do so.

❧ Specific Ethical Problems

According to religious philosopher Huston Smith, sages observing human behavior in many times and cultures have noticed that four types of activities are probable "danger spots" that need to be monitored carefully: possessions, the spoken word, violence, and sexual relations.[2] Wisdom traditions, whether Hebrew, Buddhist, or Mohammedan, develop some form of ethical code to guide and govern acceptable ways of acting in these four areas. We can immediately recognize that all four continue to be troublesome and disruptive today. How can the scriptural wisdom embodied in Benedict's Rule concerning these four areas help us to develop a spectrum of relevant and sustainable ethical values for our own day?

✑ 1. Possessions

Most of us like possessions, on the whole. In this country we generally regard property as a good thing, perhaps one of the highest values. Our legal system protects the rights of ownership even more consistently than it protects the rights of life. The founding government of the United States gave the vote only to persons who owned property—which meant only white men, since by legal definition both women and slaves were not persons but property. Our system of justice enshrines the "virtue" of ownership, and common sense suggests that only when people feel "ownership" in something will they be committed to its ongoing care.

But our cultural norms about private property are strongly at variance with the way most peoples have thought about possessions in the history of the world. For example, Native Americans were astonished and dismayed at the European colonists' assumption that land could be sold and fenced. Even today, some Asian languages do not have a personal pronoun suggesting that a thing can belong to someone for exclusive use: "mine" is an alien idea. And in Benedict's Rule, the abbot is clear about the serious danger private property presents to the human soul.

Benedict begins by stating that the abbot is responsible for all the material goods of the monastery, and he alone has authority (which may be delegated) to assign them to various monks for conservation, use, and return (RB 32). Benedict continues by questioning whether monks should have anything of their own, and states that "this vice" (private ownership) is to be "cut out by the roots from the monastery" (RB 33:1). Lest we think he does not really mean what he says, Benedict elaborates:

> No one may... give or receive anything without the abbot's order, nor to have anything as their own— not anything—neither book, writing-tablet, pen, not anything at all. (RB 33:2-3)

123

Such a spiritual discipline would likely be harder for us than fasting or keeping watch through the night. Indeed, one can imagine a full-scale revolt if such a principle were interpreted literally here and now.

In my own life I endeavor to live simply, but I recognize that Benedict's principle about no private ownership challenges me to the core. I doubt that I could do it, but even more I wonder what could make me *want* to own nothing. For example, we recently gave away about half our book collection, deciding that in many instances we could use the library instead of keeping books we rarely use. But to have no books at all of our own!—we (still) have at least ten Bibles in different translations. Can Benedict's Rule help motivate me to keep moving away from my desire to "own"?

Benedict is not objecting to possessions in reasonable measure, for the whole community of the monastery is not prohibited from owning substantial property of all kinds. He believes that the danger to the soul comes in the exclusivity of use, the temptation to hoard and to prevent others from enjoying or benefitting from what they need. Possessions are meant to serve and support our human nature, not to dominate it. Benedict well understands that in our weakness we can be dominated by things when we do not have enough, no less than when we have too much.

Benedict's approach is not the same as that of Francis of Assisi, who was committed to Lady Poverty and to living out the radical poverty of the cross. Instead, Benedict emphasizes the simplicity of the "hidden years" Jesus

124

spent in Nazareth before his public ministry began. Benedictine ownership is rooted in the common life of the *anawim,* God's little people. The principle is not so much that one must do without, for many things are granted to the community for comfort and convenience and even beauty. The principle is that all possessions are to be *shared.* This word is the key to Benedict's ethical understanding about possessions. In chapter 33 of his Rule Benedict cites as an example the earliest Christian community of the disciples after Jesus' death: "No one claimed private ownership of any possessions, but everything they owned was held in common" (Acts 4:32).

The challenge presented to us by Benedict's insight about the ethical use of possessions stands in our willingness to release control, to share what has only been lent for a time by a gracious God, to give generously from a heart filled with gratitude. I am often humbled by acts of sharing that demonstrate great freedom—a mother who never pretends her children are "hers" but always sees them as precious gifts given for her care but not under her dominion; a wealthy couple who regularly open their home for congregational events because they know themselves to be stewards of a treasure meant not just for themselves; a child who spontaneously offers a favorite toy to another. "Own nothing" for Benedictines means watch for opportunities to share; cling to nothing; let all rest lightly in your hands. Enjoy thoroughly this moment, and let the next moment bring what it will. The God who has provided so generously up until now will not abandon us in the time to come.

And this is the key to ethical use of possessions: can we trust the intent of God to provide for us abundantly? For all the reasons enumerated in this book, such trust is a very strenuous discipline for people of our time and place. And in light of what we have seen about the precipitous decline in morality among us, such trust becomes a vital link in building our common future. Is the world characterized by scarcity, so that each of us must hide and hoard in order to get our due? Or is there genuinely a possibility of abundant life, made real through the generous care of the Divine Mystery embedded in the spiritual realities of life itself? In our daily ethical choices we demonstrate which of these options we follow.

∽ 2. The Spoken Word

We have traveled a long way from the ideal of speaking only the truth. Not long ago, I found myself speechless when a friend, complaining to me that her teenaged daughter was lying to her, went on to say that she *expected* the girl would lie at school, but not at home! It is hard to imagine how we can restore the integrity of truthtelling, but as so often, Benedict's wise Rule can be of use to us.

Of several important sources of guidance in the Rule on speaking, the main one is chapter six, on silence! When words are often corrupt or destructive, perhaps the best remedy is to seek more silence. The complete title of the chapter is "Restraint in Speaking." Benedict certainly was familiar with the large biblical tradition about the dangers of speaking overmuch, and in this short chapter he quotes one psalm (39:1-3) and two proverbs (10:19 and 18:21), all to the effect that the soul can be endangered by too much talk. Currently, we are more inclined to be wary of silence than of speech. Indeed, in company with another person we seldom allow silences to occur, instead working at "keeping the conversation going."

Benedict's prohibitions against speaking are not as strict as those of other monastic rules, and the importance he attaches to scripture shows that he greatly values the Word. But his overall purpose in the Rule is to help form a community's life together in such a way that Christ is preferred above all. In order for this to happen, there must be time and space enough to listen humbly and receptively for God throughout the day. If one word can summarize Benedict's ethic of the spoken word, it is *listen*. Listen for God at all times and places. If we dispose ourselves to listen to God, Benedict hopes that our words will be formed in and through our relationship with God. Our conversation is always to be shaped by the nearness of our thoughts to God, and formed by our loving contemplation of the Truth. Benedict is reluctant to allow laughter and other boisterous behavior, which he sees as directing our focus to the very thinnest surface of reality, separating us from our awareness of God's Truth.

126

One of the three great names of God is Truth (along with Love and Beauty), and becoming the person we are in Christ requires that we are being shaped more and more by Truth's own ways. Not only are we not to lie or swear falsely, we are not to cling to deceit within our very hearts. As we draw nearer to Christ we will find that Truth itself takes up residence in us, so that when we do speak, we bring forth the truth from heart and mouth. The ethics of our truthful speech with one another is founded in the integrity of our character and our commitment to God. Thus lies, slander, false testimony, cursing, vanity, depraved speech, excessive speaking—all are sins not only against the neighbor, but also against self and God. Perhaps the best way for us to recover an ethical approach to the spoken word is to begin with a commitment to more silence in our lives, a listening and attentive silence that brings us closer to the heart of God, in which we find ourselves newly born into truth.

✂ 3. Violence

In searching for an ethical approach to possessions and the spoken word we find explicit guidelines in Benedict's Rule. However, given the importance of the next two ethical concerns—violence and sexual relations—we may be surprised to discover that the Rule itself is not explicit. We must look to the broader context of the Rule to discern its teaching in these areas.

I am increasingly concerned about violence in the Los Angeles metropolitan area in which I live. But in making that statement, I am not really speaking about anything that would show up on a police blotter. When incipient violence escalates to an actual beating or robbery or murder, the local law enforcement agencies generally handle it well. I am talking about the hostility and rage I observe at airport baggage claim carousels and freeway interchanges and department store check-out lines. I often notice the signs of incipient violence first of all in myself; it is my response to the aggression of others around me. What is violence, really? Is it war, murder, mayhem? Is it anger, rage, assault? Is it the predisposition to claim one's "rights" in every social interaction? What is encompassed by the term? This ethical issue is somewhat more ambiguous in terminology than the previous two, and yet we can see at once that it is intimately related to the overall issue of anger, or the refusing power, which was of so much concern to the monastic tradition. All that we have considered about governing thoughts of anger must be taken as background and context here.

Benedict's Rule finds its major context for all ethical issues in the gospels themselves, with particular emphasis on Jesus' teachings in the Sermon on the Mount. Especially in chapter four, Benedict reminds us of Jesus' teaching to "go the extra mile"—loving our enemies, bearing injury patiently, not returning evil for evil (RB 4:29-33). If we seek a summary of the Rule's ethical approach to violence, we can do no better than this: "Not to curse back those who curse one, but rather to bless them" (RB 4:32). The Rule suggests that confronted by violence in any form, our response should be to offer blessing in return. A one-word summary of Benedict's ethic in relation to violence is *bless.*

The Rule contains no statements prohibiting violence as such; on the contrary, it condones some "violence" we find shocking, including his comment that boys and adolescents may be denied food or whipped. Benedict places this possibility in the context of an instruction about discipline—like food or possessions—being given according to the measure of the person (RB 30). What will "reach" the disciple's will? What will best enable him to see the error of his ways? Sometimes, the conscience is not sufficiently well developed for an appeal to the understanding, and simple pain and pleasure must be the immediate remedy. The Rule makes explicit the superior's responsibility to govern everything so that the strong have something to yearn for, and the weak are not frightened away (RB 64:19). We see that Benedict is willing to use corporal punishment when he deems it helpful, but he restrains the superior's use of it more severely than do other monastic rules of his time. (See, for example, the quite remarkable sequence of punishments indicated in chapter twenty-eight of the Rule.) Benedict also makes an explicit prohibition against any monastic striking another at will (RB 70:2).

So what does it really mean to bless someone when one is more inclined to curse? On the whole, we would consider this the recommendation of a fool, for we have very little sense of the incredible power of a genuinely nonviolent response. One passage from the Rule may help illumine this, in which Benedict speaks of "the blessing of obedience," the deep blessing that arises when each of us constantly listens for Christ in all others.

> If anyone is rebuked by the abbot or by any superior in any way for however small a cause, or if he comes to believe that any superior is angered or perplexed about him, however trivially; he should

immediately and without delay cast himself on the ground at his feet, remaining there to do penance until the turmoil is healed by the other's blessing. (RB 71:6-8)

The image of casting oneself at the feet of another at the first sign of discord is strikingly similar to one from Psalm 136 used in chapter four of the Rule: instantly hurl the evil thoughts of one's heart down against the rock of Christ. Violence and evil exist, and we have no evidence that they will ever disappear altogether from this earth. Violence exists not only outside ourselves, but inside as well: sometimes we can feel the hostility rising up in ourselves eager to battle. Benedict's response is typical: notice. Be aware of what is happening within us. And as soon as awareness surfaces, immediately channel all the force of that impulse of destruction away to Christ, who will transform that power for good.

Listen again to this key phrase from the passage above: "until the turmoil is healed by the other's blessing." The commotion of violence can be transmuted into health-bringing energy through the power of love. On the whole, we do not believe this. It is amazing how completely our intelligence has been captured by the view that, in the final analysis, violent force is the strongest power that can be brought to bear, when there is so little evidence to support such a view. War never solves a problem; it simply postpones its resolution until all the parties regroup their energies. Beating more often causes hostility to simmer below the surface than brings someone around to another point of view. The only way in which peace is ever gained is through the divine power of mysterious transformation, which we can neither cause nor predict. But we *can* participate with that power through Christ by offering our blessing.

Benedictine peace is not a short-term strategy to kill off all the opposition; it is the peace of God's realm, which is different from the inherent violence even of majority rule and certainly of "might makes right." It is the peace of harmony, of delighted mutual respect, of unity celebrated in diversity. We can begin to build such an ethic of peace by learning to bless.

130

❧ 4. Sexual Relations

We are probably more confused about an appropriate ethic of sexual relations than about any other matter. From the sedate fifties we moved to the anything-goes sixties and seventies, but the longer-term consequences of an inadequate ethic of sexual relations became intolerable with the broken homes and sexual diseases and loneliness of the eighties and nineties. Dramatic shifts in the relations between men and women mean there is no going back to earlier centuries' insistence that a sexually adult woman had to be confined to the care of her father or her husband. But where and how to we begin to build a compassionate and just ethical basis for sexual relations?

Perhaps we can start with the monastic tradition's insights about lust. We all experience lusting thoughts; we all must find ways to channel them constructively; and we can trust there are such ways because God makes us as we are. The earliest monastics in the desert were convinced that the Christian life was meant to be lived as witness to something beyond what is immediately evident. For example, the desert communities fasted regularly in a world where people were starving, not to suggest that starving is a good thing for humans, but to point to the deeper truth that we do not live by bread alone. They adopted simple poverty in order to direct attention to divine abundance.[3] Central to their self-understanding were the "evangelical counsels" of poverty, obedience, and chastity based on

Luke's parable of the rich young ruler who asks Jesus how he can inherit eternal life (Luke 18:18-30).

Benedict does not adopt these three vows explicitly, although probably they are assumed in his three-in-one vow of obedience, stability, and ongoing conversion of heart (RB 58:17). But although we can be sure he understood monastic life within the overall framework of the earlier tradition, Benedict says very little in his Rule about sexual relations. He does make an interesting observation in the chapter on private ownership, that "it is not allowed that even [the monastics' own] body or will should remain subject to their own will." In other words, among the "possessions" one relinquishes in joining the monastery is one's own body. This does not mean that a disciple may be asked to do something against his conscience, but rather requires that even his vital energies be committed to the good of the common life.

131

Benedict is certainly aware that vital energies can get out of hand, and the Rule is clear on the dangers of indulging the desires of the flesh:

> Truly, as regards the desires of the flesh we believe
> that God is always present to us, as the prophet says
> to the Lord: Before you is all my desire. (RB 7:23)

And this passage points to the underlying issue—God sees all that we do. If we always act in such a way that we would be glad for God to see us, we need have no fear. Our primary purpose is the deepening and strengthening of our loving relationship with God, and our human interactions can either support that purpose or draw us away from it. Nothing is hidden from the loving eye of God.

While monastics ordinarily understand this principle to mean abstaining from sex, it need not take that form for other Christians. The basic requirement is chastity, not celibacy. That is, under God's watchful eye, our actions must always be respectful not only of those immediately affected but also of others whose lives are touched by our choices. Celibacy is the decision to abstain from sex altogether as a way of witnessing to God's all-loving nature and power. Chastity is acting sexually only when everyone is mutually honored so that Christ is preferred in all.

132

Benedictines understand that life must be vital and succulent. One famous medieval Benedictine, Hildegard of Bingen, expressed this in her concept of "greening," suggesting an image of sap flowing through the vital arteries of all living things toward joy in creation. In his Rule Benedict himself is more restrained, but even there we see the importance attributed to *passio,* powerful emotions expressed within our commitments and modeled on Christ's own wondrous loving in his final gift to us. Benedict urges us to "good zeal" (RB 72), expressed especially in our human relationships of love toward one another. We are not to be withdrawn in ourselves, dried up and sour. Instead, our lives are to be filled with fervent longing, sweet desire, and mighty care for one another.

The language the Rule uses to express the essence of our ethical obligation in all relationships, including sexual ones, is *honor one another.* In his chapters on good zeal (RB 72) and on community relationships (RB 63), Benedict turns our attention to Romans 12:10: "Outdo one another in showing honor." This is one of the primary ways in which we love God, finding Christ in every person and situation we encounter.

To honor others is to see them as God sees them, to see them as they are united with God in the fullness of their own character and commitment, to help them deepen in their development toward the persons God knows them to be. And such honor can be given to anyone at any time: the image of God is always visible for those with eyes to see. To prefer Christ in others is to see them both as people to serve (Matthew 25:35-40; RB 36:2-3 and 53:1) and as those who help us in our weakness (RB Prologue: 4). As we honor one another we support each other's weaknesses and delight in one another's strengths. The Rule's ethical standard for all human relations, including sexual ones, is to honor all (RB 4:8).

❧ Share, Listen, Bless, Honor All

Four words sum up the Rule's ethical standards in the ongoing "problem areas" of human life and relationships: share, listen, bless, honor all. If we live by these four, we are well on the way toward the foundation of a contemporary ethics that works. If we take seriously wisdom's invitation to fullness of life, as well as the importance of daily decisions to the unfolding of our own character and integrity, then we must also take seriously our ethical behavior. In a culture that disdains moral values, it is not easy to find our way toward a coherent ethical pattern. But this very brief exploration of common problem areas in human societies shows just how important our personal choices can be to the flourishing of the whole community. Courage is required to choose and act honorably when few are willing to do so. But when we ourselves are willing, we begin to notice the subtle but significant signs of radical transformation in our own lives, as well as the cumulative evidence that God is using our fullness of life as leaven on behalf of the world around us.

CHAPTER 6

Benedict and Ethics

*Not to wish to be called holy before one is so. But
first to be holy, so as to be truly called so. (RB 4:62)*

O ur ethical behavior embodies whatever we have
learned from wisdom's insight and virtue's development of character. For Christians—that is, for people who
celebrate not only the indwelling of God in the incarnation of Jesus Christ but also the Holy Spirit's indwelling
with every baptized person—there can be no doubt that
our ethics express our theology. What kind of God dwells
within us and guides our actions? How is our notion of
fullness of life expressed in our presence in the world?
Ethics is not so much a matter of outcomes, of forcing the
world to bend to "God's will," as it is a matter of relationships, of behaving in the world in a certain way
because that behavior both imitates and is empowered by
the living God. Ethics is not a matter we can "take or
leave" according to our whim, but neither is it a matter of
"testing," with God standing back and waiting to see
whether we "do it right." Instead, ethical behavior is the

way we demonstrate our love of God. Ethics is the way we reveal the living presence of God within us.

The Rule of Benedict is especially helpful as an ethical document because so many of the Rule's concerns are about everyday life—the growing, cooking, and serving of food, the balance of time in work and prayer, relationships with one another. In all these sections, Benedict shows how the gospel can be concretely lived out, how faith is expressed as an extension of worship in ordinary activities. However, the section of the Rule that is a gem of special value for ethical concerns is Benedict's chapter four, called "What Are The Instruments of Good Works?" At the end of the chapter Benedict explains:

> Behold, these are the instruments of the spiritual art. If we employ them night and day without ceasing and on the Day of Judgment return them, then these will be the wages by which the Lord will recompense us, as he promised: What eye has not seen, nor ear heard, the Lord has prepared for those who love him. (I Cor. 2:9) (RB 4:75-77)

Chapter four lists those intentions and actions by which we are to govern ourselves "night and day." The phrasing of each unit in Latin is designed to allow easy memorization of the entire list. We are meant to carry these precepts in our heart, meditating upon them, treasuring them, guiding all our choices by them. The fact that we are to "return" the instruments to God suggests that God assists us by giving us these instruments in the first place, and perhaps also gives us the capacity to employ them. The reward will be the fulfillment of our life-long, unnamable desire.

So, what *are* these instruments? What guides does Benedict gather from many sources to commend for ethical expression of wisdom and virtue? As we might expect,

Benedict begins with a restatement of three primary commands ordering the life of the faithful:

1) The commandment to love God with your whole strength, and your neighbor as yourself.

2) The Ten Commandments, incorporating the first four into (1) above and slightly amending the others to read:

   a. not to kill
   b. not to commit adultery
   c. not to engage in theft
   d. not to covet
   e. not to give false testimony
   f. to honor all.

3) The Golden Rule, stated in the form found in Tobit 4:15: not to do to another what one does not want done to oneself.

These three primary standards are foundational, occurring frequently throughout the Bible and Christian tradition. These standards are not subtle nor obscure, not hard to understand and not far away. As the book of Deuteronomy so eloquently says, "I have set before you today life and prosperity, death and adversity. . . . Choose life!" (30:15, 19). These three standards constitute the basic and essential conditions for fullness of life.

Yet if we are honest with ourselves, can *any* among us claim never to have violated at least one of them? On the whole, we are remarkably unsuccessful in our practice of these foundational instruments of good works. Why do we fail? We could attempt to excuse ourselves by claiming that we no longer accept these standards as having relevance for our lives. We could argue that coveting supports the economy, adultery is a normal release for stress, and lying is necessary for smooth social relations. We *could* make such arguments, and implicitly we often do, but are they really tenable? Even if we can justify breaking the foundational moral codes for the sake of utility or efficiency, is there no inner voice telling us that expediency is not a reliable guide to fullness of life?

This argument is not meant to suggest that there is nothing of value in experimentation, but it is meant to help us realize that character is fundamentally a matter of our own integrity, and of our relationship with God. To be people of wisdom means that we aspire to the best possible quality of life; we desire to be people who give and receive God in all our interactions with each other. The more nearly we approach God, the more aware we are of the vast gulf that separates us still from the One whom we so greatly love. We seek a quality of wholeness that haunts us by its absence.

138

By and large our world is shaped by the belief that humans are capable of being completely rational and free. We see ourselves as creators of our own self and values, able to shape ourselves and our world into the mold of our choice, capable of making and doing anything we can imagine. It is remarkable that we hold so tenaciously to this belief when it is so seldom demonstrated by the evidence. True, we have sent astronauts into space, but what have we learned about how to live in harmony with one another? The high divorce rate suggests very little progress in finding Christ in one another. True, we have the capacity to communicate instantaneously with people all over the globe, but what have we learned about how to feed the hungry? That someone still dies in the world every five seconds due to malnutrition shows appalling failure. Our insistence on the illusion that we are free and able to do the good is a way of protecting ourselves from the necessity of honestly facing our limitations.

The philosopher and novelist Iris Murdoch offers a vision of our human situation not as "isolated free choosers, monarchs of all we survey, but benighted creatures sunk in a reality whose nature we are constantly and overwhelmingly tempted to deform by fantasy."[1] The truth of our lives is seldom like an heroic adventure in which we systematically slay the external and internal "monsters" that threaten the successful accomplishment of our goals. But the reality of human contingency and ultimate helplessness is hard to bear and too often we avert our gaze rather than surrender to truth.

We fail to live according to the standards of the great commands, not because we choose otherwise but because we are not strong enough to choose life on our own. Perhaps the great commands are intended to teach us who we truly are, and what are the effective limits of our capacities. As we endeavor to follow those primary standards, we are brought again and again to the awareness that our hearts are not pure and our motives are at best mixed. Such awareness teaches us not to depend on our love of God, but instead to place our trust in God's love for us, made known especially in the life and death of Christ.

But Benedict does not pause at this point in his chapter to sympathize with our condition. Instead he pushes forward with specific actions by which we are called to live out the ethics required by the character of true life. He wants us to see in full the quality of life in Christ to which we are called.

To deny one's own self in order to follow Christ. To chastise the body: not to embrace delicacies; to love fasting. (RB 4:10-13)

The requirement to deny oneself in order to follow Christ appears in both Matthew's (16:24) and Luke's (9:23) gospels, followed by two other sentences paired with it:

> For those who want to save their life will lose it, and those who lose their life for my sake will find it. For what will it profit them if they gain the whole world but forfeit their life? (Matthew 16:25-26)

140 Obviously, the language about saving and losing is meant to thrust us into paradox, or we might say, to confuse us. Whenever we encounter an intentional paradox, we know that we are being invited to respond at some level other than thought. Paradox can only be appreciated by surrendering oneself to the heart's way of knowing.

The great problem of the spiritual life is complicated by the fact that we seem to experience everything from the point of view of an inner "I." It appears to us that we are the center of things, that we are *the* subject, the hub around which everyone and everything else circles. Whether or not we think of ourselves as important or worthy, we look out upon the world (the "other") from the "center" of our own thoughts and perspectives; everything else is experienced through the prism of self. No doubt this fact is of great value, for it enables us to be a moral agent, capable of contributing to the formation of our personality and character as well as the ongoing co-creation of the world. But the resulting image of an all-powerful "I" is an illusion. There are untold millions of such "I's," no one of whom is actually at the center of all the others. On the contrary, faith tells us that only God's very self is at the heart of the universe. And God is not someone whom we experience as tangible in the same way we experience ourselves or even other created beings.

The task of faith, therefore, is gradually to refocus our awareness so that we live and act according to the real truth of things, rather than the merely apparent truth. Thus if we center our intention upon saving our "self," the illusory thing that pretends to be in charge, we will inevitably lose not only the self, but the more important connection to God the Creator. Christ shows us the way to truthful life, and in order to follow him we must learn to deny the pretensions of the inner impostor. Language about this task is difficult because we use the word "self" to mean both the impostor-monarch as well as the unique beloved being created by God. Similarly, the word "body" refers to the skin and bone that not only "separates" us as a distinct "I" but also unites us to the universe through sensation and energy. Only when we allow ourselves to be open to the non-rational, or intuitive, knowing of our hearts, do we glimpse the truth of this troubling paradox.

141

Both Matthew's and Luke's gospels locate these three crucial sentences about dying to self in the context of a discovery of who Jesus Christ really is. Matthew 16, starting at verse 21, reads:

> From that time on, Jesus began to show his disciples that he must go to Jerusalem and undergo great suffering at the hands of the elders and chief priests and scribes, and be killed, and on the third day be raised. And Peter took him aside and began to rebuke him, saying, "God forbid it, Lord! This must never happen to you." But he turned and said to Peter, "Get behind me, Satan! You are a stumbling block to me; for you are setting your mind not on divine things but on human things." Then Jesus told his disciples, "If any want to become my followers, let them deny themselves and take up their cross and follow me. For those who want to save their life will lose it, and those who lose their life for my sake will find it." (Matthew 16:21-25)

Here Jesus has begun to teach the disciples that he must suffer and be killed, certainly a profound paradox for the Lord of Life. Peter objects, and Jesus insists that Peter harms him by this objection. In order to be his true self, Jesus must not cling to life but give it freely away.

The context for this passage in the gospel of Luke is a conversation Jesus has with his disciples about his identity:

142

> Once when Jesus was praying alone, with only the disciples near him, he asked them, "Who do the crowds say that I am?" They answered, "John the Baptist; but others, Elijah; and still others, that one of the ancient prophets has arisen." He said to them, "But who do you say that I am?" Peter answered, "The Messiah of God." He sternly ordered and commanded them not to tell anyone, saying, "The Son of Man must undergo great suffering, and be rejected by the elders, chief priests, and scribes, and be killed, and on the third day be raised." Then he said to them all, "If any want to become my followers, let them deny themselves and take up their cross daily and follow me. For those who want to save their life will lose it, and those who lose their life for my sake will save it. (Luke 9:18-24)

Here Jesus is asking the disciples who people think he is, and this time Peter affirms that Jesus is the Messiah of God. But again Jesus warns them not to let ordinary thinking distract them from the truth of full life, which inevitably involves suffering and death. We must give up those very things we hold dear, the sources of apparent pleasure and goodness, in order to find those truer pleasures in which fullness of life consists. The great "I" must be surrendered to the One at the heart of the universe. To help this happen, we are to love fasting and other practices that free us from the chains of the merely apparent, if we are to follow the path of life. Suffering is often involved, but it is not the final goal: the goal is union with Christ the beloved.

To give new life to the poor; to clothe the naked, to visit the sick, to bury the dead. To help in tribulation; to console the sorrowful. To become a stranger to worldly behavior; to prefer nothing to the love of Christ. (RB 4:14-21)

143

The fullness of life we so ardently desire is not to be hoarded, but must be given away to be enjoyed. Foundational to ethical behavior is the awareness that all living things are beloved of God, and are therefore to be respected and cherished by us. This is extraordinarily hard to do. We have so many ways of protecting and defending our privileges, not least of which is the belief that there are not enough good things for everyone, so prosperity goes to those who most deserve it. This ugly attitude can be seen in Jesus' time in the disciples' question about a blind man, "Who sinned, this man or his parents, that he was born blind?" (John 9:2), and it persists to our day, when many people assume that poverty and calamity result primarily from personal attributes such as laziness or negative thinking.

It is difficult to wean ourselves from the many disguises and protective cloaks worn by the greedy inner "I." A good beginning is active service of those in need. We are reminded of Micah's call to love tenderly and act justly—reaching out to the stranger and the sick, helping those in trouble and doing what needs to be done. Always there is risk in such service, the risk St. Francis took in embracing the leper and Mother Teresa in caring for the dying. We risk illness, danger, the loss of our own health and wealth and ease. We risk that we will be changed by those we serve.

In taking such risks we may seem odd to others, or become strangers to social convention. People may begin to avoid us, for fear that the dangers we encounter may somehow claim them as well. Among those we serve may be some who despise us for what we represent, and we may receive their scorn. Nothing is promised to those who live this way, except that in doing so they share in the life of Christ. Over time, what sustains our ability to serve is the growing awareness that we are seeing Christ everywhere and loving him in all things. We learn the secret of preferring Christ in our midst.

❧

Not to carry out anger: not to store up wrath, awaiting a time of revenge, not to cling to deceit within the heart. (RB 4:22-24)

In part two on virtue, we explored the human inclination of refusal, or anger, as a vital impulse that can be channeled to serve God. Here we see also how it can be handled in human relationships. We can direct anger outward or inward, and both are dangerous. When directed outward, it can do serious harm to others; turned inward, it is a smoldering fire that can be equally destructive. How satisfying it is to release a sudden burst of rage, but it is better to let it dissolve gradually. Even more satisfying is storing resentment inside and deliberately savoring its poison with studied attention: but better to give up such inclinations to Christ.

Ethical behavior is not a matter of suppressing unacceptable feelings. Illusion has no place in the spiritual life, and morality is not a matter of superficial pretense. The point is not that we are to manufacture some attitude we believe is socially acceptable. Instead, we begin by noticing what we are really feeling. Only when we know the truth about our inclinations are we in a sound position to choose what we want to *do* about them. Perhaps the most important insight for a genuinely ethical life is self-awareness, as, for example, knowing that some part of us would very much like to hurt those who thwart us.

Once we are aware of what is, we can aspire authentically to transcend our self-centered wishes with the help of a power beyond ourselves. Knowing ourselves, we pray for the gift of the Holy Spirit. Even before we complete this prayer, we know that God is running to join with us, empowering our loving and compassionate action. In Benedict's prologue (verse 18), we noted his awareness of God's assurance that *before* we call, God is already saying to us, "Behold, I am here." God's desire is for our wholeness, our self-transcendence in union with God.

145

Several years ago I was talking with a friend who was troubled by an overpowering rage that had laid hold of him. A colleague of his was dating my friend's ex-wife, and while rationally he knew it was none of his business, emotionally he was so upset that he was no longer able even to be civil to the colleague. He was trying and trying to get rid of the rage, but the harder he tried, the more powerful it seemed. With trepidation and prayer, I suggested that my friend set aside a generous period of time during which he would freely indulge all his rageful fantasies about the colleague—boil him in oil, tar and feather him, whatever! And when that period was ended, that he offer the whole thing to Christ, and let go of it.

My friend had to make a long drive a week later, and he did exactly as I suggested. Without sharing details, he told me that he had thoroughly enjoyed his imaginary revenge for the several hours of that drive. And afterward, to his grateful delight, the rage was simply gone and he was at peace, able to interact normally and comfortably with his colleague. Such a process is not a remedy to be employed blithely, for it is dependent for its success on a genuine desire to love and serve Christ, in which the final release to God is wholehearted. But it does emphasize that in ethical matters we are dealing with strong emotions, personal lack of freedom, and God-given transcendence.

146

> Not to give a false greeting of peace, not to turn away from love. Not to swear, lest you swear false-ly; and to bring forth the truth from heart and mouth. (RB 4:25-28)

If there is one single word associated with the Benedictines, it is "peace." Perhaps this is because of the benevolence, or well-wishing, that Benedictines so consistently offer in hospitality, almsgiving, and the arts. Perhaps it has something to do with the Hebrew *shalom,* that fullness of life associated with nearness to God. How interesting that Benedict contrasts peace with falsity. The opposite of peace, expressed in lack of ease and incipient violence toward one another, is related to the departure from truth and the embrace of falsity.

At the center of the eucharist, the greeting of peace is shared among the congregation. And Benedict says, do not give a false greeting of peace. Can one refuse to make the greeting of peace if peace is not in one's heart? What can this mean? It is not improbable that Benedict has in mind Jesus' words from the Sermon on the Mount:

> When you are offering your gift at the altar, if you remember that your brother or sister has something against you, leave your gift there before the altar and go; first be reconciled to your brother or sister, and then come and offer your gift. (Matthew 5:23-24)

At another point, Benedict makes the direct connection between worship of God and reconciliation with one another, when he requires that the Lord's Prayer be said aloud "for all to hear" at the end of the services of Lauds and Vespers "because of the thorns of scandal which are likely to spring up" (RB 13:12-13).

The ideal, the goal of ethical behavior, is not in the least diminished by its difficulty of attainment. Benedict's realism is an unfailing source of encouragement, for he never ceases to aspire to greatness simply because of the possibility of falling short. Peace is no less an important value because sometimes it is given falsely. This is a difficult concept for us to grasp. When I have tried frequently to accomplish something, never quite succeeding, I tend to turn to some other activity more likely to be satisfying. It is hard to sustain not only my effort but my enthusiasm for something that seems beyond me. And quite apart from my inner feelings, it is embarrassing to fail at my intentions so obviously in front of others. I do not like to look inept, much less to feel so.

A very simple exercise serves as a metaphor for this problem. A meditative exercise, the instructions are to breathe deeply in and out. With each full inhalation and exhalation, I am to concentrate upon a number, and nothing but that number. In the first breath, I think of "one." With the second full breath, I think "two," and so on up to the number "ten." If at any point I am distracted by *any other thought,* then I must return to the number one and begin the sequence all over again. After about five minutes of practice, the exercise is called to a halt for feedback. Usually a spirited competition ensues about who "made it" all the way to ten, along with a lot of moaning about the frequency of the necessary return to one. Astonished surprise greets the announcement that the *goal* of the exercise is not to get to ten, but to be willing to start over and over again at one! The point of all spiritual exercise is not

147

to achieve something, but to learn to wait upon God, to be present for the unexpected moment when God embraces us in full glory.

The point is not that God wants to humiliate us, but that we keep returning to the project of trying to *be God* on our own, totting up accomplishments that demonstrate our excellence, mastery, and control. And what is needed instead is that we love, love God and neighbor and self, with all the risks of vulnerability and engagement implied in loving. We are indeed meant to achieve great things, to live together in the generous bond of love that brings mutual wholeness. But the means to this goal is not our own perfection; it is rather the willingness to give up the effort to succeed on our own and the surrender to the humble work of trying again and again, each time learning more fully how to depend upon God's grace for support. Loving is never an isolated and heroic thing; it is always relational, always mutual, always interactive. Too often we avoid this truth, protecting our hearts and shielding our words in falsity in order to take refuge from the awesome demands of love.

148

Not to return evil for evil. Not to cause injury, but rather to bear it patiently. To love one's enemies. Not to curse back those who curse one, but rather to bless them. To endure persecution for justice's sake. (RB 4:29-33)

These instruments particularly remind us of Jesus' Sermon on the Mount, upon which Benedict's chapter four is roughly modeled. The Sermon on the Mount has been called the highest ethical standard the world has ever known. Yet it is only an ethical platform, a set of directives for action, it makes no sense. Recall that throughout the Sermon, Jesus brings up ethical standards of old, and raises the bar higher. "You have heard," he begins, referring to something like the proscription against murder. Then Jesus adds, "But I say to you," asking something extra well beyond the older norm, as for instance that we refrain even from insulting someone or thinking evil of them. The Sermon insists that not only the overt action, but even harsh words *or the intent to harm* are forbidden to those who would live in God's realm. This basic principle is repeated again and again.

149

If the Sermon on the Mount, or Benedict's chapter four, is purely a list of do's and don't's, it makes no sense because they are impossible to follow. All of us have impulses, feelings, instincts that cross beyond the list of "allowables" in the Sermon. If we approach it believing that Jesus' teaching sets forth conditions we must meet before we can be admitted to the presence of God, we will either despair or seek refuge in illusion.

But that is not the only way to approach the Sermon on the Mount, nor is it the only way to approach Benedict's chapter four. An alternative is to perceive with the heart that such a life is what God desires of us, such a life is what we long for at our best. But because of our creatureliness, because of our natural human limitations, we cannot live such a life unless we transcend our basic capacities. And how can anyone transcend herself? How can anyone enter his mother's womb and be born again? (John 3:4). We are invited and even encouraged to envision such foundational change because God longs to give us the Holy Spirit to help us in our weakness. We are made for self-transcendence, in intimate relationship with God in Christ. Unfortunately we have often misinterpreted our deep desires, thinking they will lead to unlimited human progress and the conquering of death and disease. The truth is more like the lesson of humility—that while we are indeed meant to be vessels overflowing with Jesus' own generosity of love, the requirement is surrendering as he did to the power of life in the God he knew.

The Sermon on the Mount is meant as an invitation to fullness of life, a life of intense intimacy with God in which our spirits are so in union with the Holy Spirit that we are able to live as light and leaven and love in the world. The ethical life is rooted in the contemplative life; love of neighbor and self become effortless when we surrender to Christ in us. The radical ethical purity sought in the Sermon and in Benedict's list of instruments is possible only in a life suffused with lively faith and trust in God. That is why Benedict's "instruments" remind us so much of Jesus' own lived experience, foreshadowed in his Sermon on the Mount. Seen as the offering of Godself to us, the Sermon on the Mount becomes real possibility.

150

Not to be proud, nor given to wine, not to be a glutton, nor given to sleeping, nor lazy, not given to murmuring, nor to speaking ill of others. (RB 4:34-39)

These instruments sound like some of the "thoughts" or vices enumerated by Evagrius and Cassian that we explored in chapter three: pride, gluttony, sloth. Verses 22-24 of Benedict's chapter four suggest the dangers in misuse of our "refusing" capacities, and here we are reminded of the problems associated with misuse of our "desiring" and "thinking" capacities. In many of his instructions throughout the Rule, Benedict expresses a conviction that how we treat our bodies has much to do with our capacity to serve God. Later chapters (39 and 40) spell out more detail about the measure of food, drink, and sleep in the monastery. Those details, together with these requirements, make the primary standard quite clear: moderation in all things. Make sure there is food all can enjoy, but not to overindulgence. Get enough sleep for the body's needs, but do not be lazy or slothful. No wine at all is probably best, but since that is too hard a standard, drink only a reasonable amount each day. Let the body and emotions support the mind and spirit, rather than gain all the attention by their reasonable or unreasonable demands.

151

Murmuring, or grumbling, is a problem of great concern to Benedict, and indeed he personally has added the second clause here about not speaking ill of others. In contrast, we would likely be disinclined to attribute much importance to grumbling, and few modern Christians would think that it caused separation from God. But Benedict insists on its importance, even though he does acknowledge that sometimes grumbling is justified when rules are arbitrary and unjust (RB 41:5), and he says the abbot is responsible for amending such practices promptly. Nonetheless, he does not condone murmuring under any circumstances.

Benedict recognizes that grumbling is a powerful ally of the internal "I-monarch" and thus an important enemy of the ethical life. The one who mutters beneath his breath is asserting his superior vantage point. If anyone knows something that might require change, it is appropriate to speak out plainly and clearly to the one in charge. But the murmurer is usually a coward, one who would rather hold on to her self-righteousness than participate in the decision process. A particularly distressing form of murmuring is speaking ill of others, with or without cause. Such action, whether gossip or libel, allows us to focus our energy and attention on the inadequacies of others rather than upon our own needs for forgiveness and growth.

152

To place one's hope in God. To attribute whatever good one sees in oneself to God, not to oneself; but always to clearly acknowledge and take personal responsibility for the evil one does. To fear the Day of Judgment: to dread hell; to desire eternal life with all ardent yearning, to daily keep death before one's eyes. (RB 4:41-47)

The more deeply one prays into this chapter, the more difficult it becomes. I have always thought that the verses about attributing all good to God and all evil to myself are particularly hard. Can't I get the credit once in a while for good behavior? Apparently the answer is "no." Benedict's instincts about the dynamics of the spiritual life prove sound again and again, as we test the Rule against our own experience in moving nearer to God. So apparently there is something unstable about the human ego, such that if it gets any credit, it will puff itself up into an exaggerated self-importance. Some tendency in us seems always eager to be "free of God" and go our own way. Thus, every time we feel the power of love moving through us, we need to teach ourselves the truth that it is power given by God. And every time we fail to love as we would, we learn again the folly of self-sufficiency.

Perhaps it feels morbid and sick to devote daily attention to the fact of our death and the impact of our current choices on what will follow. In general, the imagination is not very helpful in suggesting definitions of heaven or hell, and most of the metaphors with which we are familiar—with the exception of a few magnificent visions, like Dante's—seem trivial or punitive. The truth, of course, is that we have no idea what happens after death, until we die. So daily meditation on death probably does not mean trying to imagine what heaven or hell is like. Benedict's language does remind us that a very suitable place to focus the ardent yearnings of our hearts is on eternal life; he uses the word *concupiscentia,* which is the Latin for strong desire. Love of God is best expressed in the longing to be with God for all eternity. And also, remembering that we are creatures who will die is a powerful way of keeping ourselves aware of the contingency that marks every day of our lives and forms the basis of our self-knowledge.

153

The little verse resting quietly at the center of this chapter reveals the meaning of all the others: place one's hope in God. What a wonderful and frightening assignment this is! Many of us who have crept to the brink of awareness of the limits that bind our lives have given up on hope altogether. Others maintain the illusion of hope in progress or human achievement. To hope in God is to risk placing our whole desire for life in hands that are ambiguous and uncontrollable. Dare we take such a risk? Dare we not?

To keep custody at every hour over the actions of one's life, to know with certainty that God sees one in every place. To instantly hurl the evil thoughts of one's heart against Christ and to lay them open to one's spiritual father. (RB 4:44-50)

"Keeping custody" is a monastic custom that directly challenges our assumptions today. Vestiges of it do remain in modern religious communities where "curiosity" is still considered a dangerous practice. Science has always upheld curiosity as essential to discoveries about how things work and where they come from and what their connections are. In a positive way, curiosity is also related to wonder, the sheer delight in the awesome variety and beauty of the created world. But as always, a positive value can be overemphasized until its negative or shadow dimensions predominate. Today we frequently find curiosity to be a powerful instigator of gossip, scandal, and a source of vicarious pleasure that allows us to live through others' lives rather than our own. We may find it difficult to tear ourselves away from constant news updates on events that are emotionally stimulating but of little real value. "Custody" can be a good antidote to an out-of-control curiousity.

154

The monastic custom of "custody" can be easily observed in what is called custody of the eyes. In this practice, monastics carry out the activities of their day, moving as needed from place to place with their attention centered interiorly, perhaps focused on Abbot Issac's complete prayer: "O God come to my help; O Lord make haste to help me" (Psalm 70:1; RB 18:1). To facilitate unceasing prayer, monastics keep their gaze lowered, minimizing unnecessary visual distractions that might fragment their attention. Similarly, custody may be kept with the ears, by deliberately refraining from listening to conversations not meant for one's own ears. Custody is not considered the only appropriate way to pray, for as we have seen, monastics are often engaged in the practice of seeking Christ within all the persons and situations encountered during their day. But the two modes of prayer, coupled with the daily prayer offices, are meant to complement and support each other.

It is not easy for us to appreciate the value of keeping custody. For Americans particularly, our culture encourages an extroversion requiring a near-constant awareness of each other. Even on retreats, many people allow their attention to be significantly diluted by concern for what is happening with others. Meals eaten in silence are sometimes painful because we tend to be so poorly disciplined in the art of interior attention. And perhaps we fear the possible power of a sustained encounter with God.

But keeping custody of the senses opens us up to an expanded practice of the presence of God, with all the fearfulness and delight suggested by that possibility. And, as we have seen already, when thoughts threaten to distract us from our Godward gaze, it is a great relief to know that we may simply give them away—at their first appearance—to the trustworthy strength of our Lord Christ. Benedict reminds us that full release of temptations is often aided by finding a time to speak our thoughts aloud to a trusted elder, so that they are more readily seen as the illusions they often are.

155

To keep custody of one's mouth against depraved speech, not to love excessive speaking, not to speak words that are vain or apt to provoke laughter, not to love frequent or raucous laughter. (RB 4:51-54)

Custody of the tongue is even more important than custody of the eyes and ears. As Jesus reminds us, what comes out of us even more than what goes in reveals the true state of our hearts (Matthew 12:33-37).

Unlike some of his contemporaries, Benedict does not ask his monastics to keep verbal silence most of the time. Instead, his goal is a quality of presence to God in which all words are formed in prayer and all speech bears Christ. But he understands, too, the importance of speech as a means of human connection, and he urges monastics to encourage and support one another in their speech, even in times that call for overall silence. (See for example, RB 22:8, about arising from sleep during the great silence.) Benedict objects to laughter not because he is opposed to humor, but because he knows laughter to be so often used as a weapon against someone. Think of how many jokes are at someone's or some group's expense (mother-in-laws, ethnic minorities, people whose strange habits are "fun" to mimic). Some laughter is sheer joy, such as a child's delighted giggle at the friendly but ticklish nuzzle of a dog, but much of it is—like too much curiosity—a way of diluting our attentiveness to the presence of God.

156

> To listen willingly to holy readings, to prostrate frequently in prayer; daily to confess one's past faults to God in prayer with tears and sighs, to amend these faults for the future. (RB 4:55-58)

Although many of Benedict's instruments of good works are prohibitions, or indications of things we should avoid, there are also important items that we are actively to pursue. In particular, these four instruments are active helps, or supports, for the ethical life upon which we have embarked. And even if there are more negative commands than positive ones, the positive ones are significantly more important, as a rabbi friend used to assure me. Let us review the positively stated commands—instruments of good works—up to now in this chapter.

Love God, neighbor, and self (verses 1-2);

Honor all (verse 8);

Love fasting (verse 13);

Give new life to the poor (verses 14-19);

Prefer nothing to the love of Christ (verses 20-21);

Bring forth truth from heart and mouth (verse 28);

Love one's enemies (verse 31);

Place one's hope in God (verses 41-43);

Desire eternal life (verse 46); and

Know that God sees you everywhere (verse 49).

Out of a total of nearly fifty instruments so far, this list of ten neatly summarizes most of the others. We would do well to focus our energies and prayer for a time on these ten alone. And yet, we also find that the "negative" instruments help us understand and act upon the positive ones. So all support each other and us in our ethical development.

The four instruments in this section have to do with specific spiritual disciplines that help draw us more closely into God's own life, and thus become more receptive to the Holy Spirit's work in us. "To listen willingly to holy readings" refers to the process of *lectio divina,* either with scripture or other sacred texts, that is, praying with the text, seeking an encounter with God.[2] "To prostrate frequently in prayer" probably refers to those periods of quiet following the chanting of the psalms in the common daily offices of prayer.[3] "To confess one's past faults to God in prayer with tears and sighs" is a succinct summary of the monastic practice of compunction, or allowing the heart to be pierced by God's unmerited love.[4] And "to amend these faults for the future" is a summary of the whole monastic commitment to *conversatio morum suorum.* Here Benedict's phrase is hard to translate, but its approximate meaning is "ongoing conversion of heart," which I believe is Benedict's summary term for the themes of this book on wisdom, virtue, and ethics.[5] It would be possible to discuss these four instruments alone for a whole book, but the essential point here is that the ethical life must be rooted in the life of prayer, and monastic practice does not separate the two.

Not to gratify the desires of the flesh: to hate one's own will, to obey the precepts of the abbot in every-

thing even if he should—may it never happen!—act
otherwise, remembering that precept of the Lord:
what they say, do; but what they do, do not. Not to
wish to be called holy before one is so; but first to
be holy, so as to be truly called so. (RB 4:59-62)

158 Flesh and will here mean whatever draws us away from
God. Over and over we have seen that ethical action is
rooted above all in a profound reliance on, and cooperation with, God. A quality of willfulness and a predisposition toward immediate pleasure are characteristics that
prevent us from living life fully and well. But when we
have learned to set aside such characteristics in a joyous
surrender to God, we find that God's will is our delight.
Feeling alive and doing good become simply different
aspects of the seamless garment of wholeness.

Consider the implications of Benedict's admonition
that we not wish to be called holy before we truly are. The
sentence suggests that we are meant to become holy while
we are still alive. We might think of holiness as meaning
something *set apart* for God, like the boy Samuel who was
given to the temple as soon as he was weaned (1 Samuel
1:22-28), but a more adequate understanding of holiness
suggests that it is something *near to* God. Jesus did not
leave the community in which he was raised, but remained
in the midst of the people; yet he was in their midst as a
man wholly committed to God. Similarly, we do not have
to be set apart or separated from life in order to be near
to God, for God is present everywhere. Our intention—
our prayer and our dedication—is more important than
our location.

We do not have to be perfect in order to be holy, for
holiness does not mean perfection but relationship. We are
holy when all that we are and do happens in relation to
our ongoing bond to God. Holiness means nearness to
God, and since God is always near us, we are all poten-

tially holy. What makes the crucial difference is our awareness and our commitment to the nearness of God.

Linguistically, there is a close connection between the words "holiness" and "wholeness." A whole person is a holy one; a holy person is a whole one. We do not ordinarily think this way, but perhaps that is only because our definitions of holy and whole are faulty. Consider that the wholeness of life we so deeply desire is only possible when we become whole through the nearness of God. Wholeness is possible for human beings only when we have learned to love God with all our strength and are willing to become whole.

Still, we remain who we are. We hope that even the abbot will indeed be so holy that every action will correspond with God's precepts, but sometimes it is otherwise. Perhaps we can strengthen even our superiors by doing what they say, knowing that wholeness is what they most earnestly desire.

> Daily to fulfil in one's actions the precepts of God: to love chastity; to hate no-one; not to love jealousy, not to act out of envy, not to love contention, to flee from conceit. To reverence the seniors; and to love the juniors. In the love of Christ to pray for enemies; to make peace with opponents before the setting of the sun. (RB 4:63-73)

Again, we revisit some of the basic thoughts that Cassian warns against. Benedict has included a few additions of his own at the end of this list, from verse sixty-nine on. What links these instruments is the impact such actions have on community life. We may still believe ourselves to be isolated individuals whose free choices affect no one but ourselves, despite the growing evidence to the contrary. Especially those living in a monastery will discover all too soon the impact of envy, jealousy, unchastity, and disrespect on others' lives. Too often we allow ourselves to harbor and even nurture impulses and actions like these, without thought for their corrosive effect on the bonds linking us one to another, not to mention those linking us to God. Whatever harms another cannot fail to have its boomerang effect in our own souls. We do not pray for our enemies because we are good and they are not; we pray with tears and sighs for the hatred in us mirroring the enmity in them; and we do this only in the grace of Christ's inexplicable love for us both.

160

And never to despair of the mercy of God. (RB 4:74)

This is the final instrument of good works, and again, Benedict has made an important though brief amendment to the list he inherited. Originally this verse read, "Never despair of God," and Benedict has changed it to include a reminder of God's *mercy*. How very difficult it is to live the life outlined here! We do not want to be reminded of our own pettiness and selfish inclinations. We do not choose to think always about the fact that we will die. We do not like to see how inept and downright stupid we can be in our endless efforts to progress. We accept our dependence on God reluctantly and awkwardly. And all this in a cultural environment that implicitly considers morality to be a foolish waste of time!

How can we live in the face of this awareness without feeling foolish or being weighed down with shame and grief? We slip so quickly from thinking too much of ourselves to thinking too little. We seem to believe that we are either gods or monsters, uncertainly seeking a comfortable place to stand with equilibrium between these two extremes. And there is no permanently comfortable place to stand, because if there were we would tend to make an idol of it. We would make a golden calf, or a booth on the holy mountain, to pretend stability and certainty rather than gradually learning the flexible stance that alone keeps us alive in the vital flux of God's world. And our flexibility is born of trust in the mercy of God.

161

We return in this final tool to the insight of the midpoint: Place one's hope in God (verse 42). Do not despair of God's mercy (verse 74). It is not ourselves upon which we can rely, but God alone. Reliance does require trust, but God helps us even to trust. Despair and illusion are equally terrible alternatives. A genuine option to these prevalent temptations can only be found through a commitment to practice goodness for the sake of a vibrant and flexible faith in the living God.

> For the workshop in which we diligently use all these instruments is the enclosure of the monastery and stability in the community. (RB 4:78)

Benedict does not ask us to discover and develop these instruments on our own. Community may sometimes seem like a challenge and a curse, but it is also an enormously helpful support. It bears not only the wisdom of tradition and the daily practice of prayer, but it is also filled with others whose desires are as deep and as focused as our own. If we expect quick and easy growth in ourselves (or others), we will likely be disappointed, but we do not have to hurry. We have time, we have each other, we have God. It is enough.

May it be so for us all. Shalom and amen.

Endnotes

✿ Chapter 1: Desiring Life

1. Alasdair MacIntyre, *After Virtue* (Notre Dame: University of Notre Dame Press, 1984), 1-5.

2. For further study of wisdom, see Diane Bergant, CSA, *What Are They Saying about Wisdom Literature?* (New York: Paulist, 1984); S. Cady, M. Ronan, U. H. Taussig, *Wisdom's Feast* (San Francisco: Harper, 1986); James Crenshaw, *Old Testament Wisdom: An Introduction* (Atlanta: John Knox, 1981); R. Charles Hill, *Wisdom's Many Faces* (Collegeville, Minn.: Liturgical Press, 1996); and Roland Murphy, *The Tree of Life* (New York: Doubleday, 1990).

3. See, for example, Lawrence Kohlberg, *The Philosophy of Moral Development* (San Francisco: Harper & Row, 1981); Carol Gilligan, *In a Different Voice* (Cambridge: Harvard University Press, 1982); and James Fowler, *Stages of Faith* (San Francisco: Harper & Row, 1981).

4. Mary Margaret Funk, OSB, *The AIM Newsletter* of Mt. St. Benedict Monastery (1998), 7:3.

5. Sebastian Moore, "The New Life," in *The Way* (1984), 42.

6. C. S. Lewis, *The Weight of Glory* (New York: Macmillan, 1980), 4, 8-9.

7. Jean Piaget named various stages of child development as pre-operational, operational and post-operational. See his *Science of Education and the Psychology of the Child*, trans. Derek Coltman (Hudson, N.Y.: Viking/Penguin, 1977).

8. Aquinata Bockmann, "The Experience of God in the Rule of St. Benedict" in *Benedictines*, 51:2:7.

164

❧ Chapter 3: Developing Character

1. Jean-Pierre de Caussade, *The Sacrament of the Present Moment*, trans. Kitty Muggeridge (San Francisco: Harper & Row, 1982), 62.

2. The primary source for these concepts is much later than the period of Benedict's life: the *Summa Theologica* of Thomas Aquinas. Two helpful modern discussions of this terminology are found in Josef Pieper's *Four Cardinal Virtues* (Notre Dame, Ind.: University of Notre Dame Press, 1980) and David Baily Harned's *Patience: How We Wait Upon the World* (Cambridge, Mass.: Cowley, 1997).

3. See, for example, MacIntyre, *After Virtue*, 12-15.

4. Two recent books that discuss these thoughts well are Diogenes Allen's *Spiritual Theology* (Cambridge, Mass.: Cowley, 1997) and Mary Margaret Funk's *Thoughts Matter* (New York: Continuum, 1998).

5. Evagrius Ponticus, *The Praktikos* (Kalamazoo, Mich.: Cistercian, 1981).

6. John Cassian, *Conference* 2, trans. Colm Luibheid (New York: Paulist, 1985), 76.

7. MacIntyre, *After Virtue*, 227.

8. Allen, *Spiritual Theology*, 65.

9. Simon Tugwell, *Ways of Imperfection* (Springfield, Ill.: Templegate, 1985), 27.

❧ Chapter 4: Benedict and Virtue

1. John Cassian, *Institutes* (Grand Rapids: Eerdmans, 1986), Book 4, chapter 39. Anonymous, *Rule of the Master* (Kalamazoo, Mich.: Cistercian, 1977), chapter 10.

2. Adalbert de Vogue, *A Doctrinal and Spiritual Commentary on the Rule of St. Benedict* (Kalamazoo: Cistercian, 1983), 117.
3. Cited in *RB1980:The Rule of St. Benedict in Latin and English*, ed. Timothy Fry (Collegeville, Minn.: Liturgical Press, 1980), 196-97, footnote.
4. For further reflection on this topic, see Harned, *Patience*, especially chapter 6.
5. Adapted from an article by Wendell Berry, "Marriage Too May Have Something To Teach Us," in *Yoga Journal* (June 1987), 38-40.

☙ Chapter 5: Living with Wisdom and Virtue
1. Translation by Donal Dorr in *Spirituality and Justice* (Maryknoll, N.Y.: Orbis Books, 1984).
2. These four areas were identified by Dr. Huston Smith in a speech given on "The World's Religions as Wisdom Traditions" at the Los Angeles Philosophical Research Society in 1993.
3. See Peter Brown, *The Body and Society: Men, Women, and Sexual Renunciation in Early Christianity* (New York: Columbia University Press, 1988), chapter 11.

☙ Chapter 6: Benedict and Ethics
1. Iris Murdoch, "Against Dryness: A Polemical Sketch," *Encounter* 16 (January 1961), 20.
2. For further study of *lectio,* see my *No Moment Too Small* (Cambridge: Cowley, 1994) and *Gathered in the Word* (Nashville: Upper Room, 1996).
3. See RB, chapter 20.
4. For an excellent study of tears in the monastic tradition, see Irénée Hausheer's *Penthos: The Doctrine of Compunction in the Christian East* (Kalamazoo: Cistercian, 1982.)
5. Of the many fine studies of the meaning of *conversatio,* I recommend particularly Justin McCann's *St. Benedict* (London: Sheed & Ward, 1937), especially chapter 10; and Esther de Waal's incomparable *Seeking God: The Way of St. Benedict* (Collegeville, Minn.: Liturgical Press, 1984), especially chapter 5.

Questions for Reflection

✂ Part One: Wisdom

1. Are there people you know whom you would call wise? Are there many or only a few? What characterizes your wise friends: can you name several qualities they share? If you are so inclined, talk with several of them, asking them to talk with you about what they value.

2. Set aside a little time and place where you will not be disturbed, breathe deeply a few times, and endeavor to get in touch with that inner place in yourself where your deepest longings rest. Ponder what you find for a while, simply observing and accepting. Then take out some paper or a journal and write for about five minutes your response to the statement, "What I want is..." Just keep writing until five minutes have passed. Stop to breathe deeply again and release all thoughts. Then pick up paper and pen a second time and write something new, "What I want is..." for five more minutes. Stop to breathe deeply and release all thoughts once more. A third and final time,

take up paper and pen and write something that you have
not written before, at the truest level of yourself you
know, "What I want is..." If it helps you to do the exercise, open your Bible to John 1:38, and imagine you are
answering Jesus' question there, "What are you looking
for?" three times.

168

3. Do you have a "wisdom community"? That is, are there
people in your life who are helping you grow toward in
wisdom? This could be a group of people who know each
other and regularly meet together, or it could be several
individuals whom you know but who do not know each
other. Your actual or *ad hoc* community should be persons
who are seekers like you and with whom you can share
your deepest desires. If you do not have such persons in
your life, or have not established patterns of deep sharing
with others, think about someone you know who might
become your "wisdom friend." Is there a next best step
you could take to move in the direction of finding such
resources for yourself?

4. Discover an image or metaphor that best represents
wisdom as you understand it today. Write your thoughts
about that image or metaphor and what it might be saying to you.

5. Write your own proverb. Consider for example
Proverbs 15:17: "Better is a dinner of vegetables where
love is than a fatted ox and hatred with it." Using the
"Better is x than y" format, make up a proverb in order to
share with someone else the fruit of your experience.

✎ Part Two: Virtue
1. Standing, take off your shoes and let your feet spread
out evenly, slightly apart. Lift and stretch your toes and
then place them firmly back on the floor. Balance the

weight evenly over the whole foot, back and front, both sides. Lift through the calves and thighs, through your waist and chest, raising your arms above head. Stretch up as tall as you can. Feel the dynamic tension throughout your body. With this pose you are expressing the essence of humility in a physical stance.

169

2. What are some of the regular habits you have? Note them. What disciplined practices are part of your life now (or practices you wish were part of your life)? Note them too. Do you think of habits and practices as being quite different things? Do you think your habits influence your practices? Might the reverse also be true, that your practices might influence your habits? Is there a way you could test this?

3. For a period of about a month, commit yourself to the "discipline of gratitude." At the end of each day, consider what event or circumstance of the day just past brought you some gift, and take some time to express your thanks for what was given. Begin the next day with a return to that feeling of thankfulness, and with expectancy about what might be given this day. At the end of the month, notice if there is any change in your overall disposition.

4. Meditate on Benedict's chapter on humility over a period of some days, a few verses at a time, focusing particularly on his scripture references. Then try putting each of his steps of humility in your own words. Is there anything of value in each one that you would like to make more a regular part of your own life? Whenever you notice something that you feel might help you, make a special note of it in your own words.

5. Meditate on images of humility found in (a) the publican (Luke 18:9-14), (b) the image of ascending through

descending (RB 7:5-9; Genesis 28:12), and (c) the Magnificat (Luke 1:46-55). Perhaps talk with a few others in a small group about what they noticed and felt, and then meditate a second time on the same passage, incorporating some of the good ideas from others.

170

❧ Part Three: Ethics

1. Spend two hours being aware that everything you do or think or feel *matters*. Write down your observations afterward.

2. List about ten things that you really do not want to be done to you. Is there anything on your list that you regularly do to others?

3. Set aside some time to experiment with custody of eyes and ears while taking a walk around your neighborhood or in a quiet park. Ahead of time, decide on a comfortable distance you intend to walk. Do not rush, but also do not move too slowly. On the first walk, practice custody of the eyes, keeping your eyes soft and unfocused, aimed at a space on the ground about three or four feet in front of you. Let your ears and other senses bring information to you, but try not to raise your eyes at all. Afterward, write down what you noticed.

For custody of the ears, you might want to do a little walking with ears "tuned out"—maybe even with earmuffs or silent speakerphones on your ears. Let your other senses be as alert as you wish, but minimize auditory input. After your walk, perhaps you would like to heighten the practice by going alone to a coffee shop, and deliberately not listening to neighbor's conversations. Finally, practice custody of the ears when you are particularly bothered by an adjacent noise, say the radio of a nearby car. How much can you tune it out? Write down your observations after this experiment.

Practice keeping custody with the other senses as you wish. Then reverse the exercise, and take a walk concentrating on *receiving* from only one sense at a time: be receptive only to what you can hear, and then only receptive to what you see.

4. For the next week, whenever you encounter anything you consider violent, respond in some way that you feel conveys blessing. Notice if or how your response changes anything. In the following weeks do the same with possessions/sharing; then with the spoken word/listening; and finally with sexuality/honoring. Keep a record of your observations.

171